A GUARDS OFFICER IN THE PENINSULA

In the Spellmount/Nutshell Military list:

The Territorial Battalions - A pictorial history
The Yeomanry Regiments - A pictorial history
Over the Rhine - The Last Days of War in Europe
History of the Cambridge University OTC
Yeoman Service
The Fighting Troops of the Austro-Hungarian Army
Intelligence Officer in the Peninsula
The Scottish Regiments - A pictorial history
The Royal Marines - A pictorial history
The Royal Tank Regiment - A pictorial history
The Irish Regiments - A pictorial history
British Sieges of the Peninsular War
Victoria's Victories
Heaven and Hell: German Paratroop war diary
Rorke's Drift
Came the Dawn - Fifty years an Army Officer
Kitchener's Army - A pictorial history
On the Word of Command - A pictorial history of the
    Regimental Sergeant Major
Marlborough as Military Commander
The Art of Warfare in the Age of Marlborough
Epilogue in Burma 1945-48
Scandinavian Misadventure
The Fall of France
The First Victory: O'Connor's Desert Triumph,
    Dec 1940-Feb 1941
Blitz Over Britain
Deceivers Ever - Memoirs of a Camouflage Officer
Indian Army of the Empress 1861-1903
Heroes for Victoria 1837-1901
The Waters of Oblivion - the British Invasion of the
    Rio de la Plata, 1806-07.
Soldier's Glory - 'Rough Notes of an Old Soldier'
Craufurd's Light Division
Napoleon's Military Machine
Falklands Military Machine
Wellington's Military Machine
Commando Diary
The French are Coming! The Invasion Scare 1803-05
Military Marching - A pictorial history
Soldier On! - Testament of a Tom
The Glider Soldiers
Sons of John Company - The Indian and Pakistan
    Armies, 1903-91

In the Nautical List:

Evolution of Engineering in the Royal Nav
Vol 1. 1827-1939
In Perilous Seas
Sea of Memories

In the Aviation List:

Diary of a Bomb Aimer
Operation 'Bograt' - Memoirs of a Fighter P
A Medal for Life-Capt Leefe Robinson VC
Three Decades a Pilot-The Third Generation
Bob Doe - Fighter Pilot
The Allied Bomber War, 1939-45

A GUARDS OFFICER IN THE PENINSULA

The Peninsula War letters of John Rous,
Coldstream Guards, 1812-1814

Edited by
IAN FLETCHER

Foreword by
Lieutenant General
The Honourable Sir William Rous, KCB OBE

SPELLMOUNT LTD
Tunbridge Wells

For Deborah

© Ian Fletcher 1992
ISBN 1-873376-09-X

First published in the UK in 1992
SPELLMOUNT LTD
12 Dene Way
Speldhurst
Tunbridge Wells
Kent
TN3 0NX

British Library Cataloguing in Publication Data:

Rous, John
Guards Officer in the Peninsula:
Peninsular War letters of John Rous,
Coldstream Guards, 1812-14.
I. Title II Fletcher, Ian
940.27092

Printed in Great Britain by
BIDDLES LTD
Woodbridge Park
Guildford
Surrey

CONTENTS

ILLUSTRATIONS

1. John Edward Cornwallis Rous, later 2nd Earl of Stradbroke, in the uniform of the Coldstream Guards. (*After a painting by Thomas Beach.*)
2. The Battle of Salamanca. Fought on July 22nd 1812, it was John Rous' baptism of fire. (*After a watercolour by C. Clark, 1904.*)
3. Wellington and his staff at the Battle of the Nivelle. (*After a drawing by Thomas Heaphy.*)
4. The Guards enter France. (*After a drawing by Captain Robert Batty.*)
5. The bridge of boats across the Adour. (*After a drawing by Captain Robert Batty.*)
6. Irun. (*After a drawing by Captain Robert Batty.*)
7. The Sortie from Bayonne on April 14th 1814. (*From an engraving by T. Sutherland after W. Heath.*)
8. The portable Aneroid Barometer used by William Rufus Rous during his military career. Commissioned as ensign in the Coldstream on December 7th 1812, he was John Rous' younger brother and is mentioned in the letters.
9. The Gorget and Coldstream Stars worn by John Rous during Wellington's campaigns.
10. A Spy cartoon of the Earl of Stradbroke published by *Vanity Fair* on July 31st 1875.
11. The Earl of Stradbroke, as John Rous became in 1827. (*After a painting by A. Dixon, 1865.*)
12. Henham Hall in Suffolk.
13. A family tradition - the profession of arms. John Rous' son George, 3rd Earl of Stradbroke (seated); and grandsons, (standing from left) John, 4th Earl and Keith, 5th Earl, both Royal Navy; Peter, 16th/5th The Queen's Royal Lancers; and George, The Life Guards.
14. Lieutenant General the Honourable Sir William Rous KCB OBE and Lady Rous with their sons James (right), who has recently joined the Coldstream Guards and is at Oxford University, and Richard (left), who is at Harrow School. 10th March 1992.

Illustrations nos. 1, 8, 9, 10, 11, 12, 13 and 14 are by courtesy of Lieutenant General The Honourable Sir William Rous KCB OBE (all photographs by Jeremy Whittaker, except No.12 by Herald Photography, Blackpool.) Nos. 2, 3, 4, 5, 6 and 7 are courtesy of the National Army Museum, London, (Nos. 4, 5 and 6 are from *The Campaign of the Left-Wing of the Allied Army, in the Western Pyrenees and South of France, in the years 1813-1814*. London 1823, by Captain Robert Batty, who was with the First Guards.)

LIST OF MAPS

The maps are taken from Sir Charles Oman's *History of the Peninsular War*, (7 Volumes, Oxford, 1902-1930).

ACKNOWLEDGEMENTS

This book would not have been possible, of course, without the letters of John Rous but I must thank the following individuals and organisations who have assisted in the writing of the book; Major D.H. Toler and Major C.J. Louch (Ret'd) of RHQ Coldstream Guards, for allowing me access to the Regimental Archives; Sergeant Pearce and Guardsman Dave Milden, also of RHQ Coldstream Guards, for their help generally and for locating transcripts of the letters; the National Army Museum, for their usual good service; and Jeremy Whittaker, for taking the time and trouble to photograph the various items in possession of the Rous family.

Last but by no means least, I have to thank Lieutenant General The Honourable Sir William Rous, KCB OBE. Sir William is, of course, justifiably proud of his great grandfather and his family's rich history and apart from doing me the honour of writing the Foreword for this book, he supplied me with a great deal of additional material relating to the career of John Rous not only as a soldier but also his later life as a politician, agriculturalist and country gentleman. It is quite remarkable that a mere three generations connect John Rous, born in 1796, with Sir William and because of this he was able to provide me with information passed on by John Rous' son himself. I find this truly amazing. After editing the letters it was a great thrill to discover the existence of Rous' portrait and to finally see the face of someone who had 'lived' in the Fletcher household for so long! It was also an experience to handle the badges, shoulder plate and gorget worn by Rous in the Peninsula and the Low Countries. For this, and for his time, enthusiasm and hospitality I thank Sir William.

Below: A George III gilt jug, cast with the plaques, 'Waterloo' and 'Wellington Cup', and inscribed, 'Swaffam Races, 20th July 1815, given by the Nobility and Gentry of the County of Norfolk as a memento of National Glory. Won by Lord Rous' chestnut gelding, Araxes.' By John Harris of London, 1815.

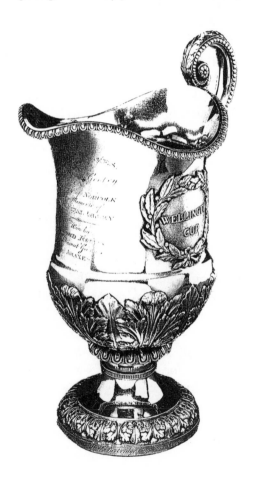

FOREWORD

By

Lieutenant General The Hon. William Rous KCB OBE

Ian Fletcher was engaged on some research into Wellington's Foot Guards from 1808 to 1815 when he stumbled across the transcripts of some letters among the archives of the Coldstream Guards at Wellington Barracks in London. These letters, the originals of which are held by the Ipswich and East Suffolk Record Office, were written by Ensign John Rous to his parents between 1812 and 1814 while he was on active service with the Coldstream Guards in Spain and Portugal during the Peninsular War. Ian was sufficiently intrigued by the story they told to edit the letters, add an introduction to each chapter to place them in their historical perspective and thus produce this most readable book, *A Guards Officer in the Peninsula*.

John Edward Cornwallis Rous, later 2nd Earl of Stradbroke, is a member of a family which can trace its history back to the Roux or Rous family from Normandy where their name is to be found on the celebrated Battle Roll in the Church at Dives near Caen. The family came to England about a hundred years before the Conquest, settled in what is now Suffolk, was later granted the hunting rights over the forests of Dunwich by William the Conqueror and has lived there ever since.

The Rouses have been active in the service of their country for generations. Some have been politicians, including Sir Anthony Rous who in 1545 bought Henham which is still the family seat and where the present Lord Stradbroke lives. Others have provided personal service to their Monarch, including Sir John Rous, MP for Dunwich when it was a flourishing port, to whom Charles II wrote from Breda on April 27th 1660 a letter which is still in the possession of the family; "....I was very well pleased with the accounts this bearer brought to me from you of the activity you have lately used for the promoting of my interests.....I hope....that I may give you my thanks in your own country. In the meantime you may be quite confident I am your affectionate friende - Charles R." And many members of the family have followed the profession of arms, including the subject of this book.

John Rous joined the Coldstream Guards in 1810 at the age of sixteen. He took part in the battles of Salamanca, Vittoria, the Nive and Nivelle, and the investment of Bayonne. At the end of the Peninsular War he returned, with the rank of Captain, to Henham for twelve months' leave but was ordered to rejoin his Regiment in Brussels following news of Napoleon's escape from Elba. John Rous experienced active service again in Wellington's campaign in Belgium and suffered an injury at Quatre Bras; some reports suggest that he was shot in the leg during the battle, others that his horse fell on him, fracturing his hip. In any event, he was sufficiently wounded or injured that, much to his frustration, he could take no active part in the Battle of Waterloo two days later. He bore a limp from this incident at Quatre Bras for the rest of his life.

John Rous left the Coldstream Guards in 1818, succeeded his father in 1827 and then pursued an active life as a peer, politician, Lord Lieutenant and Vice Admiral of Suffolk, magistrate, landowner and a man of country pursuits. He was an expert shot, a good judge of horse - better, some say, than his brother Admiral Rous who was prominent in the racing world - and most knowledgeable about greyhounds and coursing. John Rous led a most active life which is perhaps one of the reasons why he waited until he was sixty-three before marrying in 1857. He died in 1886 at the age of 92, the father of a son and five daughters. His only son was my grandfather whom I remember well when I was a small boy at Henham after the Second World War. It has always intrigued me that I knew someone whose father had fought in the Peninsula, whose father had told him all about it and who in turn was able to tell me. A long period of history is covered by a few generations of our family.

This book concentrates on a short period of John Rous' early life, but I am glad to say that mush of what he stood for then and in later years has survived, not least the Henham Estate, the family's long association with the County of Suffolk and its record of military service. On this last point, I have followed my great grandfather into the family Regiment and my elder son James likewise.

The Coldstream Guards can trace its history through more than three hundred and forty years of continuous and honourable service and it epitomises to me all that is best about the British regimental system, something which is unique to our Army and the envy of other armies throughout the world. Our regimental system is invaluable; it bestows on all those who serve under their particular capstar an inheritance which further motivates the pursuit of excellence, esprit de corps, loyalty, devotion to duty, determination and above all courage. These are war-winning qualities which an Army can only impart to its soldiers if it has been a fine Army for a very long time. The British Army has acquired precisely that reputation, earned by generations of officers and soldiers such as those mentioned in the letters which John Rous wrote to his parents when he was serving in the Peninsula.

April 1992.

Willie Rous

INTRODUCTION

John Edward Cornwallis Rous was born on February 13th 1794, just one year after the start of the twenty-two year-long struggle that was known until 1914 as 'the Great War'. Little did he know that he would be twenty-one years old before the conflict ended. During this long period Britain often stood alone as nation after nation crumbled before the armies of France, spurred on by Revolutionary fervour by the Emperor Napoleon, the 'petit corporal' who was Britain's bogey-man between the years 1793-1815.

Napoleon Bonaparte had enjoyed almost unbridled success before he took the decision to place his brother Joseph on the throne of Spain in 1808. Until this point, Napoleon stood as master of the continent of Europe and had humbled virtually every nation except Britain, the 'nation of shopkeepers', and having failed in his attempt to launch an invasion of that country, he now decided to starve her into submission by means of his 'Continental System', whereby he forbad the countries of Europe to trade with her. When Portugal failed to adhere to the Emperor's decree he ordered Junot to march into the country to enforce it and followed this a few months later by proclaiming his brother Joseph as King of Spain, thus precipitating a series of uprisings throughout both countries. Initial success led to appeals for help to which Britain responded by sending a force of some 9,000 men under Sir Arthur Wellesley to Portugal. This, ostensibly, was the beginning of the Peninsular War, a war that was to have the most profound consequences for Napoleon and a war that would see the emergence of one of the finest and certainly the most successful armies Britain has ever produced, led by her greatest ever general.

When the war began John Rous was still at Westminster School where, according to a memoir published after his death, he met men who '....cut their niches indelibly in the temple of England's

fame, and raised her prestige in war, statesmanship and diplomacy,'[1]
and it was this martial fervour prevailing at the time that induced the
high-spirited Rous to forsake a University career for the glories of
war. In June 1810, therefore, barely three months after his sixteenth
birthday, John Rous joined the Coldstream Guards as an ensign and
spent the next two years at the Regimental Depot. However, in the
summer of 1812 he sailed to Portugal to join his regiment, then
fighting with Wellington's army in Spain, taking with him his
younger brother William Rufus Rous in the expectation of getting
him an ensigncy.

      When Rous disembarked at Lisbon the Peninsular War had
reached a significant stage. The difficult early years of the war had
passed; Wellington's early successes - when, as Sir Arthur Wellesley,
he had defeated the French first at Roliça and then, a few days later,
at Vimeiro - and the consequent notorious Convention of Cintra
were almost distant memories, as was Sir John Moore's harrowing
retreat to Corunna in the winter of 1808-09.

      Having been exonerated of all charges arising from Cintra,
Wellesley returned to the Peninsula in April 1809 to lead his
developing army to victory at Oporto the following month and
Talavera in the summer of that year. But following this a year passed
without a major victory as his army stood stoutly on the Spanish-
Portuguese border defying the probing French army whilst a series
of strong defensive lines - only discovered by Massena's army when
it came face to face with them - were constructed in secret around the
Lisbon peninsula. After fighting the what in reality amounted to a
delaying action at Busaco in September 1810 Wellington's army
continued its retreat towards Lisbon.

      It was all part of Wellington's strategy but the politicians at
home, forever wary of the expenditure involved in keeping an army
overseas, were anxious as only politicians can be to get their money's
worth and soon the rumblings of discontentment began to reverber-
ate not only in the corridors of the House of Commons but also in

---

[1] The *Ipswich Journal*, Saturday, January 30th 1886.

the 'coffee houses', as Wellington called them, of the army in the Peninsula as its officers began to doubt Wellington's tactics and his ability to bring the war to a successful conclusion.

The 'croakers', as they were called, didn't make Wellington's job any easier and perhaps only a man such as himself could have weathered the verbal storm to guide his army to its eventual glorious success on wave after wave of dazzling victory. By the end of 1810 the 'croakers' complaints had become muted and early in 1811 they had been silenced as Massena's beaten and bedraggled army dragged itself away from the Lines of Torres Vedras and into Spain with Wellington's army snapping at its heels. There was a long way to go but when John Rous arrived in Lisbon in 1812 the hardest part had been accomplished.

The 1st Battalion of the Coldstream Guards had sailed for the Peninsula on December 26th 1808 and eventually disembarked at Lisbon on March 13th 1809. The regiment subsequently saw action at Oporto, where on May 12th, Wellesley audaciously crossed the Douro beneath the unwary noses of the French, carelessly watching for an advance from a different direction. Two months later, at Talavera, the Coldstream suffered heavy casualties when they pursued the defeated French division of Sebastiani too far. When they returned to the British lines, however, they gave a great cheer and later resumed their part in the fighting. The regiment also saw action at Busaco, Fuentes de Oñoro and Barrosa where Dilkes' brigade of Guards - the 2nd Battalions of the First, Coldstream and Third Guards - played a prominent part in the battle which saw the first capture by the British of a prized French eagle. It played little part in the sieges of Ciudad Rodrigo and Badajoz at the beginning of 1812 - acting merely as part of the force covering the siege operations - but took part in the battle of Salamanca in July of that year which is where we pick up John Rous's story.

The Rous letters, part of the Rous (Henham Hall) Collection at the Ipswich and East Suffolk Record Office, comprise some 32 letters in all, written by John Rous to his parents at Henham Hall in Suffolk. Although the letters may not be of the same dramatic content as some of the Peninsular journals they do, nevertheless, have a sense of immediacy about them for they were written in camp or on duty whilst on active service and were not 'tidied up' for popular consumption at a later date. Therefore, they are not tarnished by hindsight, something which often mars even the best journals, written many years afterwards when the memory had been blurred by the passing of the years.

Another feature of Rous's letters is the fact that he continued to write home from France after the war had ended, something which gives us an insight into the relationship between the defeated French and the victorious British. Some of Rous's letters contain postscripts, sometimes written as a mail arrived from England, and we can imagine him finishing off his letter as a comrade pokes his head into his tent to announce the arrival of a letter from home, causing him to re-open his letter to add an amendment or a reply to a question or point raised in the letter from England. Consequently, we are able to hear the opinions of one of Wellington's officers as the events of the war unfold as well as his often optimistic predictions. As the army settled down before the fortress of San Sebastian, a thorn in the Allied left flank as it advanced towards France, Rous wrote optimistically, 'San Sebastian will fall in five or six days.' This optimism was sadly misplaced, however, as it was to be another six weeks before the town was successfully stormed.

As befits an officer of the Guards Rous's letters reflect the manner in which only the officers of Wellington's Foot Guards could afford to live, their private incomes enabling them to procure from England all manner of luxuries and delicacies otherwise unobtainable and to sustain a relatively affluent lifestyle compared to that of the ordinary Line regiments. The Guards were indeed a cut above the rest of the army, not only because of the sheer number of lords, earls and knights - and their sons - that served with the three regiments of Foot Guards, but also because of their unique esprit de corps and the quality of their non-commissioned officers. Indeed, many years later Wellington was present at a dinner when two of the guests, who had served under the Duke, entered into a discussion on the respective merits of the Guards and the Line. As the argument became more heated Wellington was asked to give his opinion. "Oh!" he said, "I am all for the Guards - all for the Guards." Pleased at this response, one of the disputants said, "I told you so; those fellows in silk stockings and shoes have more *blood* about them, and blood will tell." "Ah!" said the Duke, "I did not mean *that*; I meant the non-commissioned officers."[2] And as if proof was needed as to the high estimation Wellington had of these he did, during the Peninsular War, recommend a score of non-commissioned officers of the Guards brigade for promotion. He is also to have said that the NCOs of the Guards got drunk regularly, but always saw that their duties had been carried out first![3]

In the Peninsula, the Foot Guards were referred to as the 'Gentlemen's Sons', for obvious reasons. They would often dine in the most extravagant manner and, as Rous says in one of his letters, "Nobody dines out without considering that fish in the first course and a roast turkey in the second is what he may reasonably expect, besides which we have plenty of woodcocks." Considering the fact that Wellington's army was often on the verge of starvation - particularly during the early years of the war when they were forced to rely on the Spaniards for provisions - this represents remarkably good living indeed.

But the Foot Guards were not considered to be Wellington's finest troops just because of the amount of blue blood that ran through their veins. They were also a highly trained and disciplined body of men and when large elements of the British army degenerated into a disorderly rabble during the harrowing retreat to Corunna in 1808-09, for example, the First Guards was one of the few regiments to maintain discipline. In fact, when the regiment came marching into Corunna at the end of the terrible retreat it did so as if on parade, with the drum major twirling his staff at the head of

---

[2] John Cowell Stepney, *Leaves from the Diary of an Officer of the Guards*, London, 1854. pp.171-172.

[3] Philip Henry Stanhope, *Conversations with the Duke of Wellington*, London, 1888. p.18.

the regiment, with drums beating and drill sergeants keeping them in step. As they came over the hills in the distance, Sir John Moore turned to Brigadier General Robert Anstruther and said, "Look at that body of men in the distance; they are the Guards, by the way they are marching."[4]

They were also a smart set of troops who took great pride in their appearance. Whereas the majority of Wellington's men preferred to improvise and wear a great deal of non-regulation clothing - out of necessity it has to be said - this practice was something which the Guards' vanity would not, unless in extreme circumstances, allow. In his *Recollections*, Captain Gronow of the First Guards, recalls an incident that happened near Bayonne in the south of France during the winter of 1813. Wellington happened to be riding past a redoubt with Colonel Freemantle and Lord Hill and as he did so was surprised to see inside the redoubt a great number of umbrellas, beneath which the officers of the First Guards were sheltering from the rain which was falling heavily. Shortly afterwards, Lord Hill came galloping up and said, "Lord Wellington does not approve of the use of umbrellas during the enemy's firing, and will not allow 'the gentlemen's sons' to make themselves ridiculous in the eyes of the army." A few days later Colonel Tynling, who commanded at the redoubt, 'received a wigging' from Wellington for suffering his officers to carry umbrellas in the face of the enemy. He also observed, "The Guards may in uniform, when on duty at St James's, carry them if they please; but in the field it is not only ridiculous but unmilitary."[5]

The Rous letters originally included gossip and titbits from home but above all contained much concerning Rous's horses in his stables back in Suffolk. His letters bemoan the fact that he will not be able to perform his duties as Steward at the Ipswich Races, he discusses the chances of his horses at the Derby and the Oaks and

---

[4] Lt.Gen. Sir F.W. Hamilton, *The Origin and History of the First or Grenadier Guards*. London, 1874. Vol.II. p.392.

[5] Nicolas Bentley, *Selections from the Recollections of Captain Gronow*, London, 1977. p.22.

often enquires as to the form not only of his horses but of his grey-hounds also. For the sake of keeping this book within the confines of the military environment in which Rous lived I have edited out most of this 'horsechat' as well as the family news but I have included his observations on the political situation at home and on the military and political situation in Europe, a subject upon of which Rous displays a good knowledge, something which also says much about the amount of literature and newspapers that was despatched to the Peninsula by friends and relatives.

In order to make the letters more readable the punctuation has been altered very slightly and paragraphs have been inserted - with paper being in such short supply such niceties were dispensed with in the Peninsula. Rous's own comments appear in brackets whereas I have used square brackets to clarify a sentence or passage. Apart from these slight modifications the letters appear much as they were written by Rous whilst on active service in the Peninsula.

Ian Fletcher, 1992.

THE PENINSULAR WAR:
CHRONOLOGY

1807

October 18th	French troops cross the Spanish frontier
November 30th	Junot occupies Lisbon

1808

March 23rd	The French occupy Madrid
May 2nd	Uprising in Madrid
July 14th	The French, under Bessières, defeat the Spaniards, under Cuesta, at Medina del Rio Seco
July 22nd	The French, under Dupont, surrender at Baylen
August 1st	A British force, under Sir Arthur Wellesley, lands at Mondego Bay, Portugal
August 17th	Wellesley defeats Delaborde at Roliça
August 21st	Wellesley defeats Junot at Vimeiro
August 30th	Convention of Cintra; Wellesley recalled to England
October 30th	The French evacuate Portugal
November 8th	Napoleon enters Spain with 200,000 men
December 4th	Napoleon occupies Madrid
December 10th	Moore advances from Salamanca
December 21st	British cavalry victory at Sahagun
December 25th	Start of the retreat to Corunna
December 26th	1st Battalion Coldstream Guards leave Canterbury for Ramsgate
December 29th	1st Battalion embarks at Ramsgate for the Peninsula

1809

January 1st-14th	Moore's retreat to Corunna
January 16th	Moore killed at Battle of Corunna
March 13th	1st Battalion Coldstream Guards disembarks at Lisbon
April 22nd	Wellesley returns to Portugal
May 12th	Wellesley crosses the Douro and captures Oporto
July 28th	Wellesley defeats Joseph at Talavera
September 4th	Wellesley is created Viscount Wellington

1810

July 10th	Massena takes Ciudad Rodrigo
July 24th	Craufurd defeated by Ney on the Coa River
July 28th	Almeida falls to the French
September 27th	Wellington victorious over Massena at Busaco
October 10th	Wellington enters the Lines of Torres Vedras
October 14th	Massena discovers Lines and halts
November 17th	Massena withdraws to Santarem

1811

March 5th	Graham victorious at Barrosa
May 3rd-5th	Wellington defeats Massena at Fuentes de Oñoro
May 16th	Beresford defeats Soult at Albuera
May 19th-June 17th	Second British siege of Badajoz

1812

January 8th	Siege of Ciudad Rodrigo begins
January 19th	Wellington takes Ciudad Rodrigo by storm
April 6th-7th	Wellington takes Badajoz by storm

June 24th	Napoleon's invasion of Russia begins
July 22th	Wellington defeats Marmont at Salamanca
August 12th	Wellington enters Madrid
September 19th	Wellington begins siege of Burgos
October 21st	Wellington abandons siege of Burgos
Oct.22nd-Nov.19th	Allied retreat to Portugal
November 19th	Allied army arrives at Ciudad Rodrigo

1813

June 21st	Wellington defeats Joseph at Vittoria, created Field Marshal
June 28th-Aug.12th	Siege of San Sebastian
July 25th	Soult makes counter-attack in the Pyrenees Battles at Maya and Roncesvalles
July 28th-30th	Wellington defeats Soult at Sorauren
August 31st	Graham takes San Sebastian by storm
August 31st	Soult repulsed at San Marcial
October 7th	Wellington crosses the Bidassoa into France
October 25th	Pamplona surrenders
November 10th	Wellington defeats Soult at the Battle of the Nivelle
December 9th-10th	Wellington defeats Soult at the Battle of the Nive

1814

February 27th	Wellington defeats Soult at Orthes
April 6th	Napoleon abdicates
April 10th	Wellington defeats Soult at Toulouse
April 14th	French sortie from Bayonne
April 17th	Soult surrenders
April 27th	Bayonne surrenders
April 30th	Treaty of Paris
May 3rd	Wellington created Duke

SPAIN AND PORTUGAL

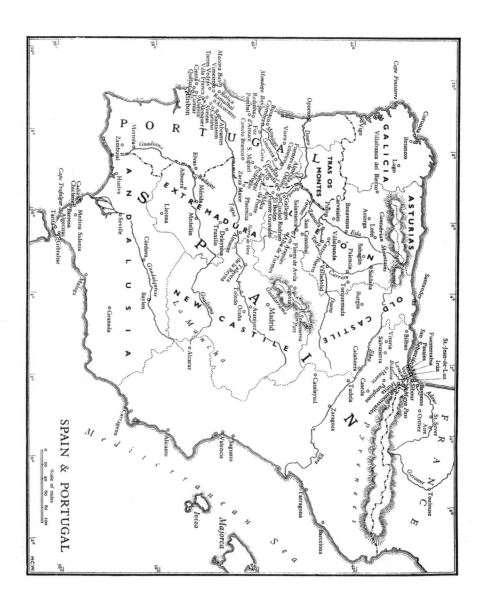

1812 - MIXED FORTUNES

1812 was a year of mixed fortunes for Wellington, beginning as it did with great success but culminating in an unhappy retreat. The first part of the year began with the fall of the fortresses of Ciudad Rodrigo and Badajoz, 'the Keys of Spain.' Ciudad Rodrigo was the first to fall, taken by storm in January 1812. After twelve days of besieging the place, in terrible weather of ice and snow, Wellington's artillery succeeded in making two breaches in the town's defences and on the night of January 19th men from the 3rd and Light Divisions moved forward in the darkness to attack the two breaches whilst diversionary attacks were planned elsewhere on the town. The fighting was hard but the assault was successful and the place taken although at a great cost to the British army. Robert 'Black Bob' Craufurd, one of Wellington's finest commanders was killed as he led his Light Division into the Lesser Breach, whilst General Henry Mackinnon, a Coldstreamer although promoted Major General only seven days earlier, was killed when a mine exploded at the Great Breach. Although the Coldstream took no part in the actual storming of the town it did take its turn digging in the trenches, a hazardous occupation in itself, involving long periods exposed to enemy fire.

With Ciudad Rodrigo in British hands Wellington's men began to slip away to the south to lay siege to a much tougher nut, the fortress of Badajoz. The plundering that took place after the fall of Ciudad Rodrigo had given the British troops a taste for more and when Badajoz fell on the night of April 6th, after another siege during which the troops tempers were further exasperated by terrible weather, that hunger was more than satisfied. However, before Wellington's men were able to give full vent to their fury they had to negotiate all manner of vicious devices placed in their way by the tenacious French defenders intent on keeping them from entering the town. They also had to weather such a storm of shot and shell as was hitherto unexperienced by them in war.

The storming of Badajoz was accomplished with an appalling butcher's bill - nearly 3,500 of Wellington's men were either killed or wounded in the assault which lasted barely three hours. Wellington himself wept when he surveyed the casualty list and the wreckage of his army in the breaches afterwards. The subsequent sacking of the city lasted almost 72 hours as the uncontrollable and battle-crazed troops gave vent to their fury and only ceased the destruction when they were too exhausted to continue. Once again the Coldstream took no part in the actual storming but was part of the covering force during the siege, preventing any interference from the French. With Badajoz securely in his hands it meant that Wellington had secured both of the fortresses that guarded the main two routes between Spain and Portugal and he could concentrate on the advance to Madrid and then the driving from Spain of the French field armies.

By now large numbers of French troops had begun to be withdrawn from Spain, bound for Napoleon's ill-fated campaign in Russia. Wellington was now offered the chance to take offensive. Having secured the fortresses he could thrust directly at Madrid, Joseph's capital. He felt that if this plan succeeded the Spaniards might at last make a properly concerted rising. Even if this did not happen Wellington could retire to his base in Portugal and try again when another chance offered.

As Rous travelled hastily from Portugal to join his regiment Wellington was about to fight one of his greatest battles. On July 22nd, just days after Rous caught up with his comrades and after days when both armies marched almost side by side, Wellington delivered a crushing blow to defeat Marmont at Salamanca. He acted with great speed when the French over-extended themselves while crossing in front of the Allied position, and thus nailed the French belief that he was simply an over-cautious and purely defensive-minded commander. It is said that Wellington was watching the French manoeuvre as he enjoyed a spot of lunch atop a hill close to the village of Los Arapiles. As he sat on his horse, 'thumping and munching' on a chicken leg, he suddenly exclaimed 'By God, that will do!' and flinging the leg of cold meat over his shoulder snapped shut his telescope and turning to Alava, his Spanish liaison officer, he said 'Mon cher Alava, Marmont est perdu!' before riding off to issue orders for a British attack.

Wellington's divisions then crossed the plain of Los Arapiles and in hardly more than forty minutes crushed more than 40,000 Frenchmen in a bloody encounter that cost the French over 13,000 men killed, wounded or taken prisoner. Amongst the wounded was Marmont himself. The battle cost Wellington 4,800 casualties, the most notable being General Le Marchant, a brilliant cavalry commander, who was killed late in the battle as he led his cavalry against the broken French infantry. It was a tough baptism if fire for John Rous. During the battle the Coldstream, under Lieutenant Colonel Woodford, held the village of Los Arapiles against repeated French attacks, a feat later mentioned by Wellington in his despatch.

The Battle of Salamanca was one of Wellington's greatest triumphs and was a turning point in the war. News of the battle spread throughout Europe, elevating Wellington's already high reputation as a military commander to an even greater standing, rivalling that even of Marlborough.

With the French army scattered and in retreat the road to Madrid was now open and on August 12th Wellington entered the Spanish capital in triumph. The year of 1812 had so far been a triumph both for Wellington and his army but the year was soon to turn sour as he embarked upon what was the most ill-managed operation carried out by the British army in the Peninsula, namely the siege of Burgos, an affair which Wellington later called, 'the worst scrape I ever was in.'

Burgos, the city of 'El Cid', was besieged in early autumn and as at Ciudad Rodrigo and Badajoz the infantry armed themselves with picks and shovels and began to dig their way towards the castle which was perched upon a precipitous slope high above the town. The various assaults on the city, including one by the Guards, were repulsed by a skilful enemy. Heavy rains set in, once more flooding the Allied trenches as they had done at Badajoz, and with a desperate shortage of ammunition and proper siege equipment - something which hampered all of the Allied sieges during the war - it soon became clear that Burgos was not to go the way of Ciudad Rodrigo or Badajoz.

The fiasco stumbled on until the repulse of another British assault on October 18th. Then, three days later, with little chance of success, with French numbers beginning to mass and threaten and having already sustained 2,064 casualties in a futile effort to take the city, Wellington decided to leave what he called 'this damned place' and during the night of the 21st the Allied army slipped quietly away to the south-west in the direction of the Portuguese frontier. All four of the main sieges undertaken by Wellington's army were less than satisfactory affairs but at least three of the were eventually successful. Burgos was the unhappiest of the lot and the misconduct of several units during the siege did not go unnoticed by Wellington who mentioned the fact in his orders but in a despatch he said the Guards carried out their duties, 'as they have every other in this army, in the most exemplary manner.'

The failure to take Burgos meant that Wellington would have to retreat all the way back to the safety of Portugal, forcing him to abandon Madrid along the way. For many of Wellington's men who had been with Sir John Moore's army three years earlier the retreat reminded them all too uncomfortably of Corunna, the army winding its way along terrible muddy roads for mile after mile, much of the time without any decent rations. The Commissariat's supply system suffered an almost total breakdown, rations became scarce forcing many men to eat acorns and it was not long before the old disease of the British soldier once again reared its head as the starving troops took to plundering in search off food as discipline broke down. Some 2,000 of Wellington's men were left to die in the mud and another 1,000 or so were taken prisoner by the French and it was an exhausted and mightily relieved army that concentrated around Ciudad Rodrigo in mid-November 1812 and settled in for the winter to re-organise itself.

However, if the retreat from Burgos was, as Wellington described it later, 'the most agonizing retreat of his career,' the year turned out even worse for Napoleon, whose defeated Grand Army totally disintegrated in the Russian snows as it retreated back to France, harassed all the time by Russian Cossacks who teased and tormented their enemies until the last French soldier had been driven from Russian soil. In fact, Napoleon's invasion of Russia had proved rather fortunate for Wellington as it meant that thousands of Bonaparte's best troops - along with vast quantities of supplies - who would otherwise have been engaged against the British and their Spanish and Portuguese allies, were withdrawn from the Peninsula to take part in the attack.

My Dear Father,   Abrantes.
                                                                July 3rd 1812.

We left Lisbon last Saturday the 27th of June, and got here yesterday.
We halted the first day at a small town about 8 miles from Lisbon,
a short march on account of our servants not understanding at first
how to pack our baggage. The second day we marched to Villa
Franca, the third day we halted at a village half way between it and
Santarem, the fourth day to Santarem, the fifth day to a small village,
the sixth day here. We halt here for one day to rest our mules and
servants. Tomorrow we proceed on our route towards Castello
Branco where we shall halt another day, and then proceed towards
Ciudad Rodrigo. Santarem is a very fine town, nothing but the walls
of the houses remaining, hardly a window to any house, which
indeed is the case with every town or village in Portugal excepting
within 3 or 4 leagues of Lisbon. The houses are all extremely filthy;
we find chiefly one chair and a table in our billets which the owners
of the house are obliged to give us. The country is beautiful in most
parts of it, the roads very bad, many places where we ride twenty or
thirty yards upon stone, like the foot pavement in London, of course
very slippery. The country agrees with me very well; the rooms are
small and smell so bad that I have slept with my shutters (for there
are no windows) open every night.
    We rise at ½ past 1 o'clock and have our baggage packed and
fairly off by ½ past 2, we then get some breakfast and start ourselves
at three. We hardly ever march after ten o'clock on account of the
heat. I slept twelve hours last night, the only good rest I have had
since I left Lisbon for we go to bed at nine o'clock. I have been very
lucky in my beasts, although they were dear;[1] I have a good strong

---

[1] The purchasing of a horse was a common practice among young officers upon
arrival in Portugal. (See Sir Charles Oman's *Wellington's Army, 1809-1814*, London,
1913, pp.269-271, for an account of horse-trading in Lisbon.) The more astute chose
to wait until after a general action when mounts were plentiful and cheaper.

Spanish horse, very quiet, I gave 200 dollars for him and if I had wished to sell him I might have 250 for him, one capital mule 130 dollars, the best I have seen yet I think, the other mule a very good one 140 dollars, and a little pony to carry William[2] till I get to the army, 46 dollars where I expect to get 50 for him. I left about £50 in Greenwood's[3] hands when I left London of my pay, and I gave the draught for the 140 dollar mule upon him. Provisions are not very dear excepting forage for our beasts; the price of it is ridiculous and very scarce from this to the army. I will write again from Castello Branco. I am bitten all over by the fleas and bugs.

Your affectionate son,

J.E.C. Rous.

[2] This was the Hon. William Rufus Rous, John's brother. Although William had been a cadet in the Royal Military College it is likely that he had come out to Portugal as a 'Volunteer'. Oman, in *Wellington's Army*, p.196, describes these as 'young men who were practically probationers; they were allowed to come out to an active service battalion on the chance of being gazetted to it without purchase, on their own responsibility.' William officially joined the Coldstreamers as an ensign on December 17th 1812.

[3] Messrs Greenwood and Cox, of Craig's Court, London. Greenwoods were army contractors who, by a definition of 1798, were 'the ordinary channel of communication between the Regiment and the Public Departments and is resorted to not only for providing and forwarding of arms, clothing and other regimental supplies but also in the business, public or private, of the individual officers.' (WO/12/4036, quoted in J.D. Turner's "Army Agency", in *Journal of the Society for Army Historical Research*, Vol.XIII. p.30.)

My Dear Mother   Castello Branco,
                                                    July 8th 1812.

We reached this place yesterday, having halted the day before at one
of the most deserted small villages in Portugal. Villa Velha contains
about four hovels inhabited by the peasants much worse than any
cottages in Suffolk, surrounded by brick walls of old houses
converted into pig sties, stables, etc. Our horses are pretty well off,
but there was no meat or corn to be bought; we made the inhabitants cut grass for our beasts and with the assistance of some eggs, our
chocolate and some porter we brought from Niza we made pretty
good cheer. Will was kicked yesterday by one of the officer's horses
severely.[1] I sent him immediately to the hospital and hope he will
be able to proceed on my pony tomorrow at ½ past one o'clock. I
have got a soldier's wife here to cook for us and we are obliged to
starve on good soup, beef-steaks, porter and wine. It is very near the
last place we shall be able to buy porter.

     Excepting my servant's accident I get on very well; I think
after tomorrow's march we shall have broken the neck of our
journey, the only thing I forgot to bring from England was a
Musketeer (I fear it is wrong spelt) Net[2] for I am bitten from head
to foot. The country generally from Abrantes is very barren, bad
road and extremely hilly (properly called mountains when writing to
a person in Suffolk). Niza resembles a large village in England more
than any town I have passed through, the streets are not narrow but

---

[1] Rous refers to his servant William Pipe. See also letter of June 20th 1813.

[2] A mosquito net was a most useful acquisition when the army found itself in
a particularly unhealthy location such as on the valley of the Guadiana or the
banks of the Caia river. Near Plasencia mosquitoes stung the officers and men so
badly that their eyes swelled until they could not see out of them. (Anthony Brett-
James, *Life in Wellington's Army*, London, 1972. p.101)

clean and it appears a healthy situation. The next place I will write from will be Ciudad Rodrigo where I shall be this day next week. I hope you will receive a letter from me dated Abrantes. It is really unfair to ask any Subaltern leaving England to carry even a small parcel for another officer; I was obliged to leave Bradshaw's[3] tea at Lisbon contrary to my wish. When you write I hope you will send me an account of what is going on in England. I have nothing to add at present excepting my best wishes to all and believe me,

your ever truly affectionate son.

J.E.C. Rous.

---

[3] James Bradshaw, 2nd (Coldstream) Guards. Commissioned as Ensign January 4th 1810, retired from the army on December 16th 1812. (Colonel Daniel Mackinnon, *Origins and Services of the Coldstream Guards*, London 1833, Vol.II. pp.510-511.)

My Dear Mother,   Marte Mayor,
                                              August 2nd 1812.

I hope you do not think I have forgotten your turn for a letter; the
case is, excepting 5 days at different times I have been on my horse
since I left Lisbon. The 1st Division halts here today and reports that
we are likely to remain 3 or 4 more but this might be counter-
ordered in a ¼ of an hour. From the excessive heat several of our
officers and men have been ill but recover in a day or two. I was
unwell 2 days ago but doctored myself without going to the rear.
     We have got (*We* means myself and Capt. Bowles,[1] an
excellent officer to live with) a room here which keeps the sun from
us, and I feel as well as I ever am, but go out only when the sun is
setting which almost everybody does when they can. I have got into
a plan of sleeping in the middle of the day, which I find necessary to
keep up my *great fatness*. We are situated here with mountains nearly
perpendicular on one side and in open country with a few small
woods on the other side and corn close to us, with a garden partly
shaded with vines, and the rest well covered with vegetables. The
town I date from and Portillia, at the top of steep hill both a quarter
of a mile distant, give nothing yet but bread and country wine,
which agrees with me very well, and will discover to you that with
the assistance of beef and mutton (the latter we have only obtained
this morning) that there is not much the matter with me now; one
day I drank nothing except tea, which I had à la Weston 3 times in
one day and ate scarcely a thing. The fact is we never drink less than
twice a day and often three times, which is the case throughout the

---

[1] George Bowles, 2nd (Coldstream) Guards. Ensign December 20th 1804,
Lieutenant February 1st 1810, Captain May 27th 1825. Bowles was made Brevet-
Major on June 18th 1815, and Brevet Lieutenant Colonel on June 14th 1821.
(Mackinnon, *The Coldstream Guards*, Vol.II. pp.508-509). George Bowles' letters can
be found in Volume II of the Earl of Malmesbury's *A Series of Letters of the First
Earl of Malmesbury, his Family and Friends from 1745 to 1820*, London, 1870.

army with those who possess dollars. The whole army has 4 months'
pay due which cannot be prevented; our officers have given from 6s
6d to 7s for a dollar, but I luckily have got remaining from £15 to
£20 worth left which will last a certain time, though nothing is sold
for less than ½ a dollar and very few things that price, I mean bread
and wine as the only things I recollect at that price.

I have written so much on the subject of eating that I have
hardly room to ask after all and to tell you that the French left 800
sick at Valladolid where we were within 5 miles yesterday and have
retired on the road to Segovia to prevent the junction with Joseph[2]
and Marmont[3] while Lord W.[4] is gone with 2 or 3 Divisions to join
[?] the Army of the Ginger Bread King, should he have the fortune
to fall in with them; The French Army will not face the British till
another Marshal arrives; you have heard of Marmont who lost his
arm in the action of the 22nd; perhaps [he] will never be able to take
any command again.[5] Although almost everybody who has been
here from two to three years is tired of campaigning I do not think
at this at the moment there are six officers in the Brigade of Guards
who would return home unless ordered, and I must repeat in this
letter that it would have been impossible for anybody to have
jumped out of the frying pan into the fire more lucky than we did.

J.E.C. Rous.

---

[2] Joseph, King of Spain (1768-1844). Born Giuseppe Bonaparte he was
Napoleon's elder brother. He was made King of Naples in 1806 and two years later
King of Spain, so precipitating the Peninsular War. He was recalled to France
following his disastrous defeat at Vittoria in 1813 and fled to the USA two years
later following the Battle of Waterloo. He died in Florence, Italy in 1844.

[3] Marshal Auguste Frédéric Louis de Marmont, Duke of Ragusa, (1774-1852).
Replaced Masséna as commander of the Army of Portugal in May 1811. He was
severely wounded at Salamanca in July the following year and was succeeded by
Clausel.

[4] Wellington is referred to throughout Rous's letters as 'Lord W.' 'the
Marquis', 'the Peer' and 'the Beau.'

[5] In spite of rumours that he had in fact been killed, Marmont had suffered
only a broken right arm.

THE SIEGE OF BURGOS

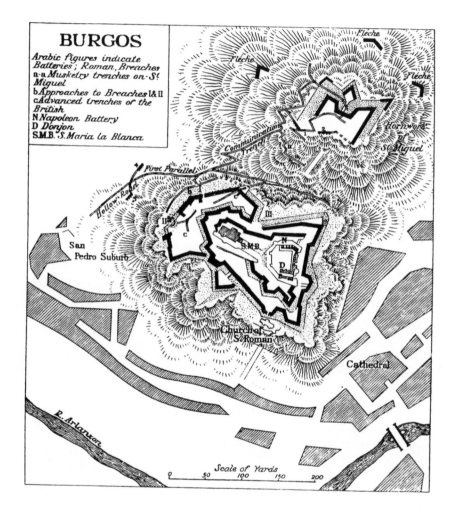

BURGOS

Arabic figures indicate
Batteries; Roman, Breaches
a-a Musketry trenches on S!
Miguel
b Approaches to Breaches I & II
c Advanced trenches of the
British
N Napoleon Battery
D Donjon
S.M.B. S. Maria la Blanca

My Dear Father   Camp opposite Tordesillas,
                                           Nov. 1st 1812.

I have at last an opportunity of writing to let you know how matters
have been going lately. We left Burgos on the 19th, having been
encamped more than a month round the town, [with] extremely bad
weather the whole time, and I may say a more unpleasant month I
never passed. Part of the 1st and 6th Divisions were always in the
trenches and my turn used to come round once in three days, twelve
hours at a time where we had the pleasure of being shot at from the
Castle without being able to return the compliment;[1] after a loss of
2500 men, we gave up the place, owing to want of *means*, having
only three 18-pounders of which two lost their trunnions. We had
worked at last close to the 1st wall, and having made a breach in it
we gained possession of it, which we maintained till we gave up the
business. Our parties were in some places within 20 yards of the
French and almost every man that was hit was shot through the
head, besides which, they rolled shells into our trenches which burst
close to us.
        The Coldstream had 3 officers killed and 3 wounded; the 3
killed were Admiral Harvey's son, Sir Bland Burgess's son and Mr.
Buckeridge. The three wounded were Lord Orford's second son who

---

[1] Duty in the trenches in front of a besieged town was a much-hated and
hazardous occupation. As at Ciudad Rodrigo and Badajoz earlier in 1812 the
infantrymen found themselves armed with shovels instead of muskets and digging
instead of fighting. This was due to the complete lack of sappers and miners in
Wellington's army, a situation not remedied until late the following year. The men
would spend long periods in the trenches, always under fire from the besieged
without being able to return it themselves and as if this were not bad enough the
atrocious bad weather endured at Ciudad Rodrigo and Badajoz made for a very
unpleasant existence. John Kincaid of the 95th summed things up in his usual
comic way when he wrote, 'One day's trench-work is as like another as the days
themselves; and like nothing better than serving an apprenticeship to the double
calling of grave-digger and gamekeeper, for we found ample employment both for
the spade and the rifle.'(*Adventures in the Rifle Brigade*, London, 1909. p.63.)

I fear will lose his arm, Capt. Fraser who will very likely lose his leg, and Capt. Crofton slightly.[2] I think myself very lucky to have escaped; the Ensigns of the Guards were on duty much oftener than anybody else owing to our battalions being stronger and our officers weaker than any other regiment. To add to this we lost 173 men - we now do not march more than 450 strong. The 1st Battalion of the 1st Regiment has joined us about 1000 strong. Their battalion is much stronger than [ours]. I had rather to go into two general [actions] than to return to Burgos, which is very advantageously situated, but could be taken in a week with 12 or 14 eighteen-pound guns. Bradshaw has left the army and is on his way to England. I have only eight Ensigns above me, and I think a year and a half more will carry me to the second battalion. The French are about 32,000 infantry and 5,000 cavalry; we are about 17,000 infantry and 1,500 cavalry.

We are now making a good and easy retreat. We shall very likely be joined by part of Hill's army, and then hope to give the French the same dinner we gave them at Salamanca, perhaps near the same place.[3] Gen. Paget[4] has joined us, and is universally liked by

---

[2] Between September 19th and October 21st the Coldstream suffered 3 officers and 54 men killed and 3 officers and 119 men wounded. The officers killed were Captain Edward Harvey and Ensigns John Buckeridge and Wentworth Burgess. Wounded officers were Captain Charles Fraser, Captain the Hon. William Crofton and Captain the Hon. John Walpole. (Mackinnon, *Coldstream Guards*, p.179.)

[3] Rous's letter was written some ten days into the retreat from Burgos and the 'good and easy retreat' was soon to turn into what Wellington called 'the worst scrape I was ever in.' As the rains turned the roads into quagmires hundreds of British soldiers were left to die starving in the mud as the Commissariat broke down. For many it bore too close a resemblance to the retreat to Corunna just over three years earlier. The army eventually concentrated on November 15th at Salamanca where Wellington offered battle at the same place as he had on July 22nd. Soult, however, botched his chance, much to the anger of the rest of his army; Wellington's retreat continued and a glorious opportunity went begging.

[4] Lieutenant General Edward Paget (1775-1849). Commanded the rearguard during Moore's retreat to Corunna. He had returned to the Peninsula having lost his right arm three years earlier during the Crossing of the Douro. He was captured shortly after his arrival during the retreat from Burgos.

the officers and must soon be so by the rest of the men, since whatever is liked by the former is always so by the latter, at least in regiments like the Guards. We are encamped on stony ground and dined last night upon a piece of mutton that had marched 5 leagues the same day, and was no sooner killed than put into the pot. There appears no chance at present of going into cantonments.

I dined about a fortnight ago at Headquarters where the Marquis gave us as good a dinner as is found in England and was in good spirits. We have been terribly off for forage lately, our mules have had very long marches and more than once [there has been] nothing to be got when they come in till the next morning. They are all miserably thin and I have had the pleasure of seeing my animals literally starving. I sold one of the mules I bought at Salamanca which was stolen two days afterwards, and my bay horse being so much out of condition I have bought a brown horse and shall try and sell the bay. I have regularly forgotten to let you know that I have not found the least difficulty in getting money since I first joined the regiment, but have been obliged to give 5s.9d. for every dollar worth only 5s. owing to the great scarcity of money.

I bought a nice tent for 15 guineas at a Sale the other day.[5] Bradshaw is a great loss to us;[6] he was generally reckoned a clever, good tempered man and had he been a poor man without any other prospect than his profession would have made a good officer. He lived at great expense here, I think he could not have spent less than £1000 a year which he did not make go further than most people do £700. In England he will certainly run through his fortune, but

---

[5] Such sales were usually held as a result of the death of a fellow officer. While his more sentimental and valuable possessions might be sent to his family other personal items such as his baggage, equipment and weapons were sold by auction and after deducting possible funeral expenses the proceeds of these often melancholy affairs usually forwarded to his family. (For an account of one such auction see *The Private Journal of F. Seymour Larpent, Judge-Advocate General, attached to the Head-Quarters of Lord Wellington during the Peninsular War, from 1812 to its close.* Ed. Sir George Larpent. London, 1853. Vol.II. pp.72-73.)

[6] Ensign James Bradshaw returned home to England and resigned from the army in December 1812. (See note no.2 of letter dated July 8th 1812)

luckily he dislikes Play and will never ruin himself - his ideas are those of going beyond anybody else, which £4000 a year and keeping no accounts cannot possibly do. I have not yet seen William's name in the Gazette; he is exactly the age to enter the army. We have been very busy lately and shall be so for some time, when we get into quarters (if we do this year). We expect 5 or 6 officers from our 2nd Battalion immediately. With love to all, believe me,

Your very affectionate son,

J.E.C. Rous.

THE REGION BETWEEN
SALAMANCA AND ALMEIDA
Illustrating the retreat of November 1812

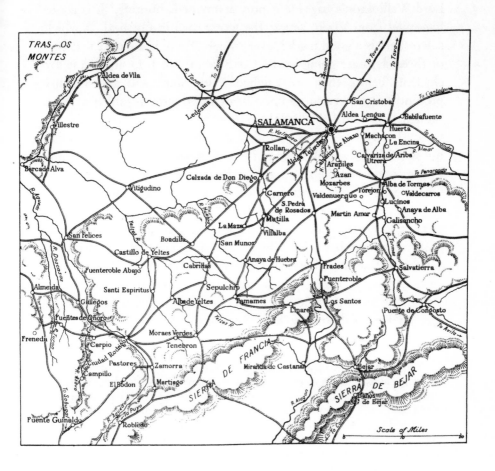

My Dear Father,   December 10th 1812.

I fear there will now be some difficulty in getting my letters into
Lord Wellington's bag. He is now at Freineda hunting.[1] It is about
five miles from Vizeu, almost the worst road in Portugal, at which
town there is a good market every week. There is a report that two
or three steps are going in the Coldstream, but I do not count my
chickens before they are hatched. Nine steps will give me my
promotion, and I calculate upon being in London in June next year,
though I am told I shall be there sooner.

In my letter to my Mother I have stated the reason for my
not wishing to have William in the Coldsteam, and at the same time
I have mentioned the advantage of the Guards. The First Brigade of
Guards is at Vizeu consisting of the 1st and 3rd Battalions of the 1st
Regiment. Our Brigade which is called *the Brigade*, is much the
greatest favourite with the Peer; upon the arrival of the former at
Duennas where they joined the 1st Division, Lord W. said that they
were very fine men, but that there was something in the dirty old
coats of the old brigade which he, Lord W. preferred.

We have had accounts from General Paget who was unfortunately taken in the retreat from Salamanca.[2] A French officer states

---

[1] Fox hunting was a popular pastime at Headquarters and Wellington, a good
equestrian himself, could often be seen galloping frantically behind the hounds in
pursuit of 'the uneatable'. George Bowles, Rous's living companion, wrote, 'He
[Wellington] will certainly break his neck some day.' (Malmesbury, *A Series of
Letters*, Vol.II. p.240.) The Coldstream Guards, in fact, even supplied a huntsman,
Tom Crane, who appeared dressed in a long bright scarlet coat. (Anthony Brett-
James, *Life in Wellington's Army*, p.200.) In fact, whilst hunting near Freineda the
hounds chased a fox into French territory and both Crane and the pack were
captured. The French, however, ever mindful of the Britons' sporting instinct, sent
them back the next morning under a flag of truce!

[2] Sir Edward Paget was captured by a French patrol from Vinot's light cavalry
on November 17th. He was riding without escort and when attacked was unable
to defend himself having lost an arm at Oporto in 1809. He had only recently
arrived in the Peninsula to assume his post as second-in-command of the army.

him as being 'bien triste'; I fancy they could not get anything out of him. He at first refused to give his name and rank, but was very soon recognised by a French officer who recollected seeing him Oporto, just before Soult's retreat from that place in 1809.

They say that Lord W. is coming to this place to install Mr. Stuart, Knight; he is English Minister at Lisbon.[3] The Palace of this town belongs to three or four brothers who live magnificently; it resembles an English mansion in every particular and is much the finest house in Portugal. It is fitted up with English beds, etc.

The Horse Guards and Blues are at Lisbon. I think there will be a scarcity of officers in the 10th Light Dragoons, should they continue only to do London duty. A veteran battalion is about to be raised at Lisbon consisting of soldiers and officers who have become unfit for service in this country. A detachment of 100 men which left England in July to join this battalion only joined us yesterday; six weeks ago they were at Benavente, but hearing that some French Dragoons were near them, they were obliged to retire by Braganza where they halted a fortnight to receive Orders. Only 54 have joined; 11 men stopped behind one day and missed their road and 35 are gone sick to Lisbon; the 1st Battalion of the 1st Guards which left England 1200 strong do not muster more than 600 on parade, the 3rd Battalion in the same proportion; they sent above 20 to Hospital on one day. I am expecting a mail every day; it will be rather interesting when it arrives. With kind remembrance to all at home. I remain.

Your truly affectionate Son,

J.E.C. Rous.

---

[3] Charles Stuart (1779-1845) succeeded John Charles Villiers as British Minister to the Council of Regency in Lisbon. Stuart's father, General Sir Charles Stuart, had commanded the British troops sent to Portugal in 1797 during the Second Coalition.

1813 - TO THE PYRENEES

The winter of 1812-13 came and went and by the spring of 1813 Wellington's army was strong enough again to begin the offensive that would take them across Spain, over the Pyrenees and into France. Moreover, he would advance to the Pyrenees in the knowledge that not only had Napoleon's Grand Army suffered a terrible reverse in Russia but the Allied army's of Russia, Prussia and Austria were advancing in the north, an advance culminating in the defeat of Napoleon at Leipzig on October 16th-19th.

As Wellington advanced, this time taking Burgos without any trouble, Joseph pulled back his forces first from their positions on the Douro, then Burgos and finally from the Ebro. His army was somewhat reduced in size owing to the withdrawal of many of his troops who had been sent to join the Emperor on his disastrous Russian adventure. At Vittoria, however, he could still count on a sizeable number of French troops, he himself commanding some 66,000 while Clausel was expected to join him from Pamplona. But even as Clausel was marching to Joseph's assistance Wellington's men were marching grimly through the wild and rocky country of the Cantabrian mountains, hauling their guns across ravines and over terrain considered impassable to artillery by the French.

On the misty morning of June 21st Wellington's army burst from the hills surrounding the plain in front of Vittoria. One by one the divisions were fed into the action by Wellington and by five o'clock in the afternoon, after fierce fighting, the French forces finally buckled under the weight of the relentless Allied attacks. Joseph was forced to give the order for a general retreat which precipitated some of the most astonishing scenes of the whole Peninsular War as the retreat turned into a total rout. The French suddenly degenerated into a helpless mob and in their panic Joseph and his staff left behind them all their artillery, huge quantities of supplies but more amazingly a baggage train containing a vast quantity of booty which amounted to well over a million pounds.

In the streets of Vittoria, jammed solid with baggage waggons and other discarded army equipment, the French had been forced to abandon all but two of their 153 guns, as well as 415 caissons. Over 2,000 prisoners were also taken. As well as the immense amount of treasure taken, the British also inflicted some 8,000 casualties on the French while suffering 5,000 themselves. It was a magnificent victory and as a result Wellington was given the rank of Field Marshal.

With the French army brushed aside at Vittoria the Allied push towards France ground onwards and soon only the rugged mountains of the Pyrenees lay between Wellington's army and the 'sacred soil' of France. However, before the advance could continue there were still two pockets of French resistance, holed up behind the walls of the strongly-fortified towns of Pamplona and San Sebastian. These were a potential threat as they lay on both right and left flanks of the Allied army and would have to be snuffed out before any thoughts could be turned to crossing the Pyrenees.

However, even as Wellington's troops began to besiege San Sebastian on June 28th, Marshal Soult was planning a bold counter-attack through the Pyrenees in order to relieve both Pamplona and San Sebastian. On July 25th he launched two attacks, at the passes of Maya and Roncesvalles. At Maya a fierce fight ensued but the pass remained in French hands in spite of a British counter-attack that checked any further French advance. The action cost the French 2,000 casualties and the British 1,500, as well as four guns, the first and only occasion that Wellington lost a gun.

Whilst the French were attacking at Maya a similar offensive was underway at the pass of Roncesvalles. As at Maya the fighting was heavy and conditions difficult on the steep slopes of the pass. The outnumbered British force held on until late afternoon when the pass was shrouded in a thick mist that came down suddenly. The British commander, Cole, lost his nerve somewhat and withdrew his force from the pass despite specific orders from Wellington not to do so and he retreated along the road to Pamplona.

At the end of the day neither French attack had proved decisive, although Cole's unauthorized withdrawal from Roncesvalles placed Wellington in some danger. The outcome of the two attacks did not deter Soult who made another attack three days later, this time at the village of Sorauren. By now Wellington himself had arrived, having rode over from his headquarters at Lesaca, and he narrowly avoided capture by French dragoons as he sat writing a despatch on the bridge in the village. As he rode up to the top of the ridge occupied by the British and Portuguese troops, the latter, recognising instantly the figure of the commander-in-chief, began to chant 'Douro! Douro!' which was taken up by the British troops. The ominous chanting bode ill for the French and sure enough when Soult made a strong attack on July 28th he was driven off leaving Pamplona even more isolated.

Towards the end of August another of the unhappy episodes of the Allied campaign in the Peninsula drew to a close as the siege of San Sebastian reached its climax. On August 31st, the town fell - after the loss of some 2,376 casualties - to Thomas Graham, commanding the British and Portuguese troops there. The assault on the town was quite remarkable as the main assault got underway in daylight, unlike the usual method of going in after dark. Allied losses were heavy; 856 killed and 1,520 wounded and once again there followed the same disgraceful and shocking scenes that had marred the successes at Ciudad Rodrigo and Badajoz, this time made worse by a fire that engulfed the town and left hardly a building standing. The Coldstream supplied 55 men for the storming party, over half of whom became casualties during the assault.

By the autumn of 1813 Napoleon's situation was growing more desperate. His forces were defeated at Leipzig by the combined armies of Austria, Russia and Prussia - Britain was represented by a unit of the Rocket Troop - and even as their armies began to move steadily west towards France Wellington was preparing to drive the French armies across the Pyrenees and out of Spain. On October 7th his men crossed the Bidassoa river in a masterly operation and with the capture of the Greater Rhune, an important position in the fight for the Pyrenees, Wellington's men, after five years of hard slog, found themselves fighting on French soil for the first time.

Pamplona fell on October 23rd and as the November rains fell, turning the roads into mud, Wellington prepared to carve even deeper into French territory. The Brigade of Guards saw much action as Wellington's army fought its way out of the Pyrenees. On November 10th he fought the Battle of the Nivelle which forced Soult to retreat to the line of the River Nive. Once established in France Wellington was to give the retreating French army little respite. On December 9th his men advanced towards Bayonne and two days later, following their victory at the Battle of the Nive, they were laying siege to the place. With the onset of winter and with his army firmly in control of the situation around Bayonne Wellington paused to plan the final thrust that would be made early in 1814.

My Dear Mother,   Mongualde,
                                            January 11th 1813.

My not having received a letter from Henham by the last two mails
leads me to conclude that some mistake is the cause of it; the
regulation of the post here is extremely bad, sometimes we do not
receive our letters till two days after the arrival of them at Vizeu,
which place, by the by, I have not given you any account of. I rode
over to see it, about a fortnight since, and it is unquestionably a
better sort of Portuguese town than any I have seen yet. The houses
are large, the streets rather narrow but clean; the people are very well
affected in favour of the English. The town is nearly if not quite as
large as Ipswich, there is a Fair every tuesday and a market every
day.

Fish is to be got in plenty, which I can assure you makes a
great addition to our dinner. Nobody dines out without considering
that fish in the first course and a roast turkey in the second is what
he may reasonably expect, besides which we have plenty of woodcocks. This is merely to give you an idea of the living of the Guards
when compared with that of the Line, who live on a pound of tough
beef and a pound and a half of bread (per diem) commonly called
ration, a thing not known with us when in quarters.[1] But I fancy

---

[1] This outrageously haughty passage from the aristocratic Rous surely
epitomises the Guards approach to campaign life compared to that of the Line
regiments. It has to be said, however, that only the Guards, with their private
incomes, could afford to maintain such a good lifestyle in the field and indulge in
such culinary delights as Rous mentions throughout his letters. That the Guards
lived an often lavish lifestyle is born out by the tale of an officer of the 1st Foot
Guards, the Hon. W. Dawson who had brought from England 'innumerable
hampers of wine, liqueurs, hams, potted meat, and other good things,' as well as
a host of cooks. So lavish a table did he keep that even Wellington himself dined
with him on one occasion. Unfortunately, Dawson's income was unable to keep
pace with his appetite and he was eventually obliged to quit the Guards. As
Gronow put it, 'his friends had literally eaten up his little fortune.' (*Selections from
the Reminiscences of Captain Gronow*, ed. by Nicholas Bentley, London, 1977. p.16)

that good living causes good soldiers, for I believe nobody will deny that the Guards are the finest troops in the world, and the longer William remains with them the more he will feel the benefit of having begun his military career in so well disciplined a corps.

I have had no promotion since I left Burgos; our Captains fancy that a peace is likely and therefore ask larger sums than they would otherwise.[2] I must beg leave to apologize for having written so careless a letter; I have had a return of my ague, which with calomel at night and bark in the daytime has left me. Percival[3] is recovering from a severe attack of the rheumatism, which confined him to his bed some days. I am sorry to hear of Bonaparte's arrival at Paris. Lord W. is at Lisbon. Mr. Stuart, the English Minister at that place is to be knighted. The Peer is to install him.[4]

I saw an account in the paper of Lord Anson's son being killed by accident on board the 'Baccante'. With love to all believe me,

your truly affectionate son,

J.E.C.Rous.

---

[2] Basically, at the time of the Peninsular War promotion in the British Army was usually by either purchase or by the filling of a vacancy within the regiment by the senior officer of the next lower rank. There was, of course, liable to be plenty of vacancies in a regiment on active service due to death, wounds or sickness and it made sense to wait for such an opening rather than waste money on purchasing a commission. If peace was in the offing, however, vacancies would again be scarce and the prices asked for consequently high, hence the shrewd business move on the part of the Coldstreamers' captains, not a cheering prospect for the ambitious officer with limited means at his disposal.

[3] George Harvey Percival, 2nd (Coldstream) Guards. Former Gentleman Cadet at the Royal Military College. Joined Coldstreamers as an Ensign, March 16th 1809; Lieutenant, March 25th 1813. Died November 11th 1815.

[4] See note no.2 of letter dated Dec.10th 1812.

My Dear Mother   Mongualde,
                                                        March 15th 1813.

We have not yet got the mail which contained letters from the date
of January 28th to February 4th. You have without doubt expected
letters from me long before this will reach you, but having been
three months at this place there is no news, and I write now merely
to let you know I am quite well. I do not think we shall march for
three weeks. I am afraid I shall be ordered to Vizeu on Thursday
upon a general Court Martial which is likely to last some days. It is
upon 24 Poles belonging to the German Legion who deserted and
have been since taken. They were made prisoners at Badajoz and
volunteered to serve in the German Legion.[1] Percival will start for
Lisbon to join the 2nd Battalion in a few days; he will be in London
about the first week in May. I see in the army list that William has
one below him in the Coldstream.[2] My stud is now in very good
order. My horse and three mules are worth £130 or £140.

   I have desired Hatchard to send me regularly the Quarterly
Review;[3] I shall be obliged to you to find out from Col. Fuller[4] the

---

[1] These Poles were evidently taken prisoner following the storming of Badajoz
on April 6th 1812. The King's German Legion was formed in 1803 and originally
consisted of Hanoverian exiles who had come to England to fight against
Napoleon. They acquitted themselves with great honour in the Peninsula and were
perhaps the most reliable and able of Wellington's foreign auxiliaries. However,
the Poles - not to mention most of the many soldiers of the French army who,
following capture, volunteered to serve in the Allied army - owed little allegiance
to their new masters and often took the first opportunity available to them to
desert to their former comrades, a fatal course of action if subsequently recaptured.

[2] ie. another Ensign in the Coldstream.

[3] Hatchard's was and still is a major London bookseller. The Quarterly Review
was founded in 1809 and had John Murray, Walter Scott and Robert Southey
among its leading writers.

[4] Lieutenant Colonel Joseph Fuller, 2nd (Coldstream) Guards. Commissioned
as Ensign, Aug.1st 1792; Lieutenant, Jan.22nd 1794; Captain-Lieutenant, June 18th
1801; Captain, May 25th 1803; Major General, June 4th 1813.

best way to get it sent to the army. It is the best plan to send all my letters to the Orderly Room and then I fancy none of them pay postage. If there should be any books come out in London which it is the fashion for everybody to read I wish you would send them here. Lockwood[5] tells me he has forwarded my Horse Physic[6] to Lisbon, I think I should have heard of it from my father in the letter I fancy is lost. Pray remember me to all and believe me to remain,

Your truly affectionate Son,

J.E.C. Rous.

---

[5] Lieutenant William Lockwood, 2nd (Coldstream) Guards. Lockwood was with the 2nd Battalion in England.

[6] This is s confusing reference. At first glance one would assume that Rous is referring to a vet. However, as no further mention is made of it in his letters and taken in context with the preceding passage I can only assume that the 'Horse Physic' in question was, in fact, a book, several of which had been published dealing with the horse's anatomy. However, there were a small number of veterinary surgeons present with the army. (See Ernest A. Gray's *The Trumpet of Glory: the military career of John Shipp, first veterinary surgeon to join the British Army.* (London, 1985), for a fine account of the very first vet.) Cavalry horses were usually treated by farriers and I think it very unlikely that Rous had his own personal vet, something which, for an infantry officer, would have been extravagant even for an officer of the Guards!

My Dear Mother,   Mongualde,
                                                                April 11th 1813.

I received yesterday your letter of the 22nd of March. I have changed
my house here for a larger; we have now two good rooms with fire
places, two middling ditto without, a good kitchen, besides an ante-
room; *we* means Capt. Bowles and myself who have lived together
ever since I joined. I believe you recollect seeing him at the exhibi-
tion of pictures in Pall Mall two years ago. I am rather forgetting my
French. The only reason I wish for peace is that I should like going
to France for 3 or 4 months. I get on pretty well in Portuguese. I am
most happy to see Mr. Whitbread[1] has been set down by his own
Party; he has committed himself most entirely, but does not like to
own it. I see no chance of my being in England before June next
year. I am not anxious to return, particularly if I could go on the
staff, but I know no Generals who want aides-de-camp.

Everybody here is of your opinion respecting the Princess of
Wales being an unfit companion for her daughter, but almost all
defend her, some for the sake of abusing the Prince - others think her
an injured woman. For my part I do not believe half of what Lady
Douglas swears to, but have no doubt that Her Royal Highness is
the worst person the young Princess can live with. I am at present
on a Court Martial at Vizeu upon an Ensign of the Coldstream, for
an unlucky circumstance which took place before he came into the
regiment, when he was in the 68th.[2] At present it is going on well,
I am only sorry that he exchanged into the Coldstream before the

---

[1] Samuel Whitbread (1758-1815) was M.P. for Bedford. A Radical, he was
instrumental in reforming the Poor Law. He was opposed to the war, however,
and was disliked for his anti-war stance, his policy eventually leading to a split in
the Whig party. He committed suicide in 1815.

[2] William Kortright, who joined the Coldstream as an Ensign from the 68th
Regiment on November 26th 1812. He remained with the regiment until promoted
to Captain in the 93rd Regiment on September 11th 1817.

Court Martial was over, since in the four years the Guards have been in the Peninsula there has been no instance of any officer or soldier having been brought to a General Court Martial,[3] and although everybody that chooses may know that he was not in the Guards at the time the circumstance took place, many of the Line will not know it through envy.

I am very sorry to see the account of the Amelia frigate; I know from the little experience I have had in this country, that French soldiers are as brave as it is possible for men to be, particularly their Officers; at the same time it is mortifying to our Navy to hear of a French frigate fairly beating an English although the French frigate was rather of superior size. I would never compare soldiers with sailors particularly when the English sailors are allowed to be the best in the world, but our soldiers certainly have been gaining great advantage over the Americans.[4] I should very well like to go to Germany[5] but I fear that none of our Royal Dukes are capable of commanding an army, or of doing any good at Hanover. I should be for giving it to Bernadotte,[6] for the French or Swedes can take it if

---

[3] This is not strictly true. Recorded in the archives of the Coldstream Guards are many instances of soldiers having been brought before Courts Martial for misconduct in the Peninsula.

[4] The War of 1812 between Britain and the USA had broken out mainly as a result of a trade dispute between the two countries. The 'great advantages' that Rous refers to came early in the war, a conflict in which the British had marginally the best of the land actions including the burning of the US capital, Washington, by veterans from the Peninsula, released as the war there drew to a close. The final decisive battle, however, at New Orleans in January 1815 resulted in a crushing defeat for them at the hands of Andrew Jackson's Americans. The British commander here was Wellington's brother-in-law, Edward Pakenham, who was killed during the battle.

[5] The German Campaign or War of Liberation as it sometimes known expelled the French from Germany for good and culminated in the Allies defeat of Napoleon at Leipzig in October 1813.

[6] Jean-Baptiste Jules Bernadotte (1763-1844). Served with distinction under Napoleon and was created Marshal of France. However, Napoleon dismissed him from the army following the Battle of Wagram in 1809. The following year he became Crown Prince of Sweden and three years later, following Napoleon's seizure of Swedish Pomerania he found himself fighting on the opposite side of his

they like. There is no news here. With kind remembrances to all, believe me to remain,

Your very affectionate Son,

J.E.C. Rous.

---

old master as commander as the Army of the North in the German campaign. He became King Charles XIV in 1818 and his dynasty still exists today.

My Dear Father,   Lamego,
                                                 May 15th 1813.

We have at length left Mongualde and are moving on the road to
Braganza and from thence it is supposed we shall march towards
Burgos. The 3rd and 5th Divisions are with us besides Gen. Pack's[1]
and Bradford's[2] Brigades; in all about 20,000 infantry and 2 or 3,000
cavalry, German and Portuguese. This Corps is to be under the
command of Genl. Graham[3] who is at present sick at Freineda and
will be here in a few days, this will be the army of the left flank;
Lord W. will have the 4th, 6th, 7th and Light Divisions on our right;
Genl. Hill[4] will have the 2nd Division, General Hamilton's Division[5] and some other Portuguese Corps on the right of Lord W.,

---

[1] Major General Sir Denis Pack (1772-1823). Served in Flanders, Ireland, the
Cape of Good Hope and South America. Commanded a Portuguese brigade in the
Peninsula where he was wounded eight times. He was also wounded at Waterloo.

[2] General Sir Thomas Bradford (1777-1853). Like Pack he also served in the
abortive South American campaign of 1806-07. He served in the Peninsula and
from 1810 commanded a Portuguese brigade. He was badly wounded at Bayonne
in 1814.

[3] General Sir Thomas Graham, Baron Lynedoch (1748-1843). While returning
to England through France following the death of his wife, French revolutionary
guards searched her coffin looking for arms. So outraged was Graham that he
raised the 90th Regiment of Foot at his own expense and began an almost personal
crusade against the armies of France. He triumphed at the Battle of Barrosa in 1811
and commanded the 1st Division of Wellington's army for the following two
years. He commanded at the siege of San Sebastian and later founded the United
Services Club.

[4] General Sir Rowland Hill (1772-1842). One of Wellington's most trusted
generals. Known to the troops as 'Daddy' Hill - he always looked to the welfare
of the troops under his command - he commanded the 2nd Division from 1809-
1814, and the right wing of the army for the last two of these years. He was Commander-in-Chief of the British Army from 1828 to 1829.

[5] Lieutenant General Sir John Hamilton (1755-1835). Was made Inspector-
General of the Portuguese Army in 1809 and commanded a Portuguese division
at Albuera and on the Nivelle.

and the Alicante Army will form the right flank, under Gen. Murray.[6] This appears a formidable force and we have to oppose about 60,000 men the French have concentrated near Valladolid besides Suchet's[7] army and some other small corps. When we have driven them behind the Ebro we must take Burgos and Pancorbo, that being done we can cross the Ebro and try to drive them out of Spain. We have been so long at Mongualde that the people were sorry to part with us. Several women have followed the Regiment.[8]

You mentioned in your last letter that my tailor had sent in a Bill for clothes I had of him before I left London. I am not aware that I owed him one shilling and I think my Mother must have the receipt. I wrote word in my last letter that I had only six Ensigns above me, but a Colonel who we all thought had sent in his resignation has called off therefore there are 7 above me and unless we have pretty sharp work this year which there seems every chance of, I shall not get my promotion for a year and a half. I had reckoned upon being in England next June year. The 1st Guards are at Oporto and unless they recover very fast they will take very little share in this campaign. The Coldstream are at present about 500

---

[6] Major-General Sir John Murray. Commanded the Anglo-Sicilian detachment at Alicante. He later abandoned all of his guns and equipment which had been landed for the siege of Tarragona and re-embarked without telling the Spaniards whom he shamefully abandoned. He was court-martialled in 1815 but was acquitted of most of the charges.

[7] Louis Gabriel Suchet, Duc d'Albufera da Valencia (1770-1826). Saw service in Spain from 1808 until the evacuation of eastern Spain in 1814. He commanded the French army in Catalonia from 1811, when he was made a Marshal of France, until 1814. As Wellington advanced to the Pyrenees Suchet proved a constant threat to his right flank.

[8] Wellington's army was followed throughout the war by all manner of loose women and sutlers, eager to relieve the soldiers of their pay. There was, of course, a large number of army wives who marched with the army. No more than six wives per company were allowed to go abroad with their husbands, drawn by lots the night before a regiment embarked. It was always a very tense moment as the tickets marked 'To go' and 'Not to go' were drawn from a hat and while the lucky ones celebrated there was intense grief amongst those who would be left behind to face an uncertain future at home and probable starvation.

men; we expect to get a draft of 130 men tomorrow or the next day and nearly 50 more are coming up from Lisbon. I shall hope to hear all the news of the Newmarket meetings and the Derby.[9] Pray remember me to all and believe me to remain,

Your truly affectionate Son,

J.E.C. Rous.

---

[9] John Rous was a great lover of horses and greyhounds. Although the many references to his animals have been edited out it is worth mentioning his most notable horse, 'Quiz', the Stradbroke racehorse, who won seventeen races including the 1801 St. Leger. A fine portrait of him by Henry Bernard Chalon (1770-1849) is in possesion of the family today.

My Dear Mother,   Camp near Bercianos,
                                                      May 28th 1813.

The 1st Division are encamped near the village of Bercianos which
is about eight leagues from Braganza and nearly the same distance
from Benavente. We heard yesterday that 1500 French cavalry were
at Benavente but they have most likely made off today. The French
have a garrison at Zamora, and excepting that garrison which it is
necessary to send to England I do not expect to see any Frenchmen
till we cross the Ebro. Lord Wellington is moving by the old route
to Salamanca and Valladolid and Gen. Hill has passed the Guadarra-
ma. Gen. Graham is expected to join us in two days; he will have the
command of a very fine corps of more than 20,000 British and
Portuguese and from 12 to 18,000 Spanish infantry besides nearly
5,000 cavalry of three nations.

       This is a year in which the people in England may expect
much to be done.[1] Lord Wellington commences this campaign with
a larger force of infantry (besides having command of Spanish troops)
and the same number of British cavalry than he did last year. The
French have not more than 2/3 the force they had last January year
and I think as soon as we have taken Burgos and Pancorvo in the
north of Spain and if the whole army are able to cross the Ebro, we
may expect to drive our foe to the Pyrenees. There are several strong
places to be taken on the other side of the Ebro such as Vittoria,
Pamplona and others, but should we be forced to winter on this side
of the Ebro, the continuance of the war here, I think ought to

---

[1] Indeed, after the difficult early years of the war and the setback of the retreat
to Burgos - coming as it did after the successes at Ciudad Rodrigo, Badajoz and
Salamanca - the British politicians and public demanded victory. Wellington
himself knew that he would have no better chance than he had at the outset of
1813, the more so since nearly 30,000 French troops had been withdrawn to take
part in Napoleon's ill-fated Russian Campaign. Wellington, on the other hand,
commanded 'a larger and more efficient army than I have yet had.'(*Despatches of
Field-Marshal the Duke of Wellington*, London, 1834-39. Vol.X. p.240.)

depend on the reinforcement which France can send to her army and that will be decided by the operations of the Russians and Prussians in Germany this year.[2] It appears certain that Bonaparte must give up Spain or Germany provided that the Prussians and Russians remain true to their cause; if he is wise he will give up Spain for an army like the allied army in Germany is more to be feared than 20 countries like Spain peopled by such lazy wretches as the Spaniards or such profound vain cowards as the higher classes, not that it is fair to find much fault with the character of a Spanish soldier. He wants nothing excepting to be well-drilled and commanded by a Spanish officer who has the spirit and energy of a British, German or French officer; the Spanish peasantry are perhaps the finest looking men in Europe, they have too much pride to be commanded by foreigners and no confidence in their own noblemen. The use of the Spanish troops who are with us, will hope that in case of an action they will occupy a space in line and after victory they may be sent to butcher the unfortunate wounded which just suits their character and is in fact only a retaliation for what the French did when they entered Spain.[3]

I cannot describe to you the long faces and lamentations at Mongualde the day we left it. Our soldiers having been some time in the country are reconciled to the manners of Portuguese and never

---

[2] In fact, as early as January of 1813 Wellington had received news of Napoleon's disaster in Russia. The implications were of course, that there would be little chance of any reinforcements being sent to Spain. On the contrary, it seemed likely that troops would be withdrawn from the Peninsula instead and sent to assist in Germany.

[3] It is almost universally agreed by Wellington's men that unlike their Portuguese counterparts the quality of the Spanish army was poor and the quality of its officers poorer still (at Talavera the Spaniards ran away at the sound of their own musketry!). Of the Spanish officers William Surtees of the 95th said, 'most of them appeared to be utterly unfit and unable to command their men....the most contemptible creatures...that I ever beheld.' (William Surtees, *Twenty-five Years in the Rifle Brigade*, Edinburgh and London, 1833. pp.108-109.) The Spanish people, on the other hand, were full of spirit and resistance while the guerrillas did great damage, tying down thousands of French troops that might otherwise have been employed elsewhere against the Allied army.

stay anywhere long without becoming associates with its inhabitants; our train of washer women is nearly triple what it was last December. I have not received any letters from you for some time but I hope we shall receive another mail in a week or so. With kind remembrance to all. Believe me to remain,

Your very affectionate Son,

J.E.C. Rous.

My Dear Mother,   Sotresquedo,
                                             June 12th 1813.

I should apologize for not having before given you a more accurate
account of the natives of Spain and Portugal and I am afraid you
fancied that the officers of this army live a great deal with the
inhabitants; the fact is that we see as little of them as it is possible.
The greatest people in large towns are shopkeepers and Justices of
Peace and in villages they are all of one class namely peasants. When
we go into quarters we generally dive to the extremity of their
information in two hours which seldom extends beyond being able
to inform us, how long it is since the French have left them and
what mischief they did before they went, and they cannot always
give an accurate account of this; but whether Spain and Portugal is
a Continent an Island or a Peninsula is far beyond their comprehen-
sion. Of other countries they have little or no idea farther than
knowing there are such countries as France and England; this is
decidedly the case in Portugal excepting in Lisbon and Oporto at
which places the whole Nobility and all landowners reside who did
not succeed in flying to the Brazils at the time the French were so
near Lisbon.[1] In Spain it is nearly the same thing, but owing to
there being more large towns in Spain the Nobility are more
scattered.

At these large towns Lord W. gives Balls to amuse the people
there;[2] but officers doing duty with their regiments seldom or never

---

[1] When Napoleon's troops entered Portugal in 1807 to enforce his 'Continental
System' the Portuguese royal family of Prince Don John fled to the Portuguese
colony of Brazil, sailing in November of that year just as Junot's troops entered
Lisbon, leaving the country in the hands of a Council of Regency.

[2] Wellington was a great giver of balls and as the Guards' regiments were
usually to be found close to his Headquarters their officers, contrary to what Rous
says, were frequently in attendance. A wide range of excuses was given for these
balls, such as the anniversary of a battle, the king's birthday and other special
events. (See Brett-James, *Wellington's Army*, pp.167-171, for accounts of such balls.)

partake of these amusements, in short excepting my trip to Oporto I have not been to a Ball since I left Lisbon and shall very likely never go to another till I get to England, of which there appears no prospect for some time to come. If I pay for letters it is charged in my account at Greenwoods, I am not certain; at all events I hope that will be no impediment to your writing often even if it did cost ten times what it does. You will see by the place I dated my last letter from how much advanced we are since I wrote last. We are now about 6 leagues to the left of Burgos; some of the Divisions are at Burgos, and our idea here is that the Peer intends to leave it and cross the Ebro as soon as possible.

At present we have outmarched our Commissariat and are under the necessity of going without bread for a day or two till it can come up. They are baking at Palencia and at many of the villages near here. We have halted today after a march of 12 days without halting and nothing but the want of bread prevented our progress today. I hope whatever is sent out to me will not be sent to Lisbon since there is no possible way of getting any from thence. I hear that Ministers have promised Lord W. drafts to the amount of 10,000 men to keep this army at its present effective strength which is 75,000 infantry, which includes 12,000 Spaniards, besides about 7 or 8,000 cavalry. We have had a great deal of wet weather lately but our men being under tents at night prevents the sickness which would otherwise have been occasioned.[3] Adieu and with best love to all.

Your very affectionate Son,

J.E.C. Rous.

---

[3] Although tents had been issued to a few regiments in the Peninsula it was not until the beginning of the 1813 campaign that tents were made a general issue for all British infantry regiments, one for each field officer, one for the company officers, one each for the adjutant, quartermaster, the medical staff and the paymaster. For the NCOs and men three tents per company were issued. (S.G.P. Ward, *Wellington's Headquarters, A Study of the Administrative Problems in the Peninsula, 1809-1814*. London, 1957. p.200.)

My Dear Mother,   3½ Leagues from Vittoria,
                                                      June 20th 1813.

The immense tract of country we have passed over during the last
month will I trust be a sufficient excuse for my not having written
oftener; for the last week we have always marched at 4 o'clock am
and not halted on our ground for the night till nearly six o'clock
pm, in addition to the pleasure of this we have had an unusual
quantity of wet weather and the men have had flour instead of bread;
in fact our army never before experienced what we have lately, at
this season of the year. I am now writing while the men are cooking
but we expect to march in an hour. 5 days since we marched at 4 in
the morning and did not halt till half past 12 at night, we then
marched at 5 and did not halt until 3 o'clock.

   We have had two successful skirmishes in which we have
taken a great deal of Baggage and altogether about 1,000 men; I have
not time to enter into any detail, but the papers will most likely give
you the most accurate description. Our army is in the highest order
and we may reasonably expect a short, brilliant, and decisive
campaign. Our whole army is within 4 Leagues and the French are
at Vittoria and on this side of it; we seem to think that they will
form a junction with Suchet. We have lately passed over a very
mountainous country for which reason the French will not retreat
any further than they are obliged.[1] We must have a day's halt in a
short time, in which case you may depend upon my writing.

   There are papers arrived up to the 3rd from London, but I
have not yet had an opportunity of seeing them. I have heard the
report of an armistice between the Russians and the French which is

---

[1] The country to the west of Vittoria is indeed a very mountainous region and
made for hard marching for Wellington's infantry. In fact, the French considered
the country virtually impassable to artillery and were quietly confident of
withstanding Wellington's army. However, a series of forced marches through the
mountains eventually won the day for him.

to last from the 4th of June till the 5th of July.[2] The French here have ordered all their women and officers wives back to France besides some of their heavy baggage; this will have a great effect upon the people of Bayonne. The 1st Guards are still at Oporto, where I hope they will remain the whole year; they have seen three retreats and have never seen an advance; we fancy that their appearing is the omen of bad luck. Their promotion is very rapid and if they should join will be much more so, there are still many left who cannot undergo this sort of fatigue.

I have only time to say that I am in good health; there is an order just come to move off in one hour. I saw W. Pipe two days back who is living with an officer of the 18th Dragoons, I feel rather interested that he should turn out better than he promised to when he left me which was my reason for trying to get him a good place.[3] I must now wish you goodbye and with my best love to all, believe me to remain,

Your truly affectionate Son,

J.E.C. Rous.

---

[2] Following his victories at Lützen (May 2nd) and Bautzen (May 20th-21st) Napoleon negotiated an armistice to last until August 16th. However, when news of Wellington's victory at Vittoria reached them the Austrians, under Metternich, decided to join the Coalition against Napoleon and used the truce to prepare for war. Austria officially declared war on France on August 12th.

[3] William Pipe, Rous's former servant. See also letters of July 8th 1812 and September 17th 1813.

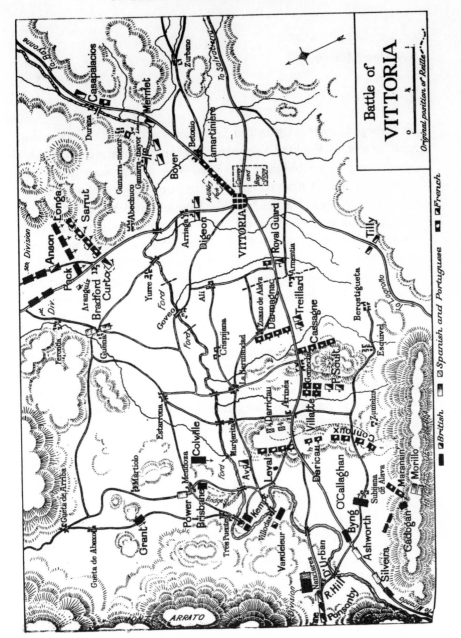

Battle of
VITTORIA

Original position of Railte

My Dear Mother,   Irun,
                                                      July 3rd 1813.

Sir George Collier is off to San Sebastian and intends to send a ship
with letters to England tomorrow morning, I therefore take this
opportunity of scribbling a few lines. You will be surprised to see
from what place I have dated my letter, only three miles from San
Sebastian and three leagues from the frontier town Yrun [Irun]. I am
not sure I have spelt Yrun or Ernam right, but the places are spelt
so on Faden's map.[1] Lord W. is at Pamplona; I believe he has not
settled whether we shall besiege it regularly or only mask it.
    I believe Suchet is out of Spain; the main French army under
Joseph which we bullied so much at Vittoria is fairly in France, and
the inhabitants of Bayonne are packing up to retire into the body of
the country.[2] We are occupying the line of country from this place
to Pamplona and so downwards to Sir John Murray and in fact
saving the garrisons at San Sebastian, Pamplona and one or two other
places we have fairly driven the French to their own country, a task
which many people in England denied the possibility of our
accomplishing, and which by the masterly style in which Lord W.
has performed it, shows that he is much improved as a General since
last year, and that owing to the long period that he has commanded

---

[1] A good map of the Iberian Peninsula was essential for Wellington's officers,
most of whom would write home asking for one to be sent out to them. The best
and most widely used ones were printed by William Faden and D. Tomás López.
Faden's map consisted of four sheets which when pasted together, 'would fill the
whole side of a moderate-sized room'. The López map, which was printed in
London by Faden, was the basis of all maps of Spain available at the time of the
war. (Ward, *Wellington's Headquarters*, pp.104-106.) William Napier was prepared
to pay up to 20 guineas for a copy of the latter. (*Life of General Sir William Napier*,
ed. by H.A. Bruce, London, 1864. Vol.I. p.109.)

[2] Following his defeat at Vittoria Joseph had been stripped of his command
and recalled to France. He was replaced by Napoleon by Marshal Soult who
assumed command on July 1st.

a British army in this country he has become without doubt the first General of his age.

After the Battle of Vittoria we went through some very severe work owing to the wet weather and not having any rations of biscuit; we were five days in arrears, but there were scarcely any grumbles amongst our men who seemed to be aware of the consequence of pushing on, and the impossibility of the Commissariat department keeping up with us. We are now however regularly rationed and most of the Division are got into houses today. The unusual quantity of wet weather we have had for some time does not seem to decrease nor is there any chance of doing so at present. The first fine day I mean to ride to Irun then to cross the Bidassoa merely to say I have been in France. The Spaniards are in front and I have no doubt do not spare the people on the other side of the river. The Spaniards here are very anxious that we should march into France to allow the Spanish troops to revenge the wrongs that Spain has felt for the last six years but that is out of the question.[3]

I have received no letters of later date than May 24th or thereabouts, but I hear that two mails have arrived at Pamplona. Pray remember me to all at home, and believe me to remain,

Your very affectionate Son,

J.E.C. Rous.

---

[3] The Spaniards' desire for revenge after years of French occupation is understandable but it was vital for Wellington to maintain the discipline of his army lest there spring up a French resistance movement similar to that organised by the Spaniards themselves. After the crossing of the Nivelle there was so much plundering and pillaging of French towns and villages by the Spaniards that Wellington was eventually obliged to send them all back across the border and into Spain, all, that is, except for Morillo's well-disciplined division of 4,500.

My Dear Father,   Camp near San Sebastian,
                                                        July 18th 1813.

I received your letter of the 14th and one from my Mother of the 1st
of last month; Gen. Graham has papers of the 5th of July in which
I understand Lord W. is made a Field Marshal for his victory at
Vittoria.[1] His Lordship's dispatch is the most curious I ever read,
and was written I dare say in a great hurry; he does not give the
number of killed, wounded and prisoners on either side. According
to the most accurate information I can procure the loss of the allied
army was about six thousand men, of which number 400 were
Spanish and about 1,200 Portuguese; we took about 1,200 prisoners
and 200 pieces of artillery instead of 151.[2] The last 50 were found in
the woods and narrow roads a week or ten days afterwards. Lord W.
also mentions the capture of one gun near Pamplona where we killed
about 300 men and the French entered Pamplona with one howitzer
only, being the sole field piece of 200 intended for preventing out
taking possession of the Pyrenees.

The 1st Division returned to this place yesterday to assist the
5th in the siege. We have been for some days in position about one
league from the frontier town, but since there appears little probability of the French returning into Spain for the present we are in the

---

[1] After his victory at Vittoria Wellington had sent the baton of Marshal
Jourdan - which had been captured along with a vast amount of plunder after the
battle - to the Prince Regent who in turn raised him to the rank of Field Marshal.
'You have sent me among the trophies of your unrivalled fame,' wrote the Prince,
'the staff of a French Marshal, and I send you in return that of England.'
(Elizabeth Longford, *Wellington - The Years of the Sword*. London, 1969. p.323.)

[2] Actual French losses were 42 officers and 714 men killed, 226 officers and
4,188 men wounded and 23 officers and 2,801 men taken prisoner or listed as
'missing', making a total of 8,008. The French also lost 151 guns, 415 caissons and
100 artillery waggons. 'Probably no other army ever left *all* of its artillery save two
pieces in the enemy's hands.' (Sir Charles Oman, *A History of the Peninsular War*,
Oxford, 1922. Vol.VI. p.442.)

meantime to have the benefit of another siege, but I trust very different from the last we were engaged in. I was on duty from 11 o'clock last night till 7 this morning being unluckily the first for duty on our arriving here, as I was also at Burgos last year. The Engineers always boast at first sight that they will take a place in six or seven days; they have just found out that this place is very strong, but we have a magnificent Train and I hope we shall accomplish our undertaking in five or six days more.[3]

I forgot to mention in the commencement of my letter that the French loss was nearly equal to ours; our having taken so many guns was the reason that our loss was more severe than it would otherwise have been.[4] Lord Bentinck[5] has taken command of the Alicante army and Suchet [is] retiring. [We hear] that Gen. Sir J. [Murray] will be Court Martial[led]; it appears that his behaviour in retreating to his ships was unwarrantable, and proves him to be as great an ignoramus as many people supposed he was after he had written the foolish dispatch in the end of April or beginning of May last.[6]

---

[3] Rous was being very optimistic here. San Sebastian proved to be yet another of the disappointing sieges in the Peninsula. The first assault on the town on July 25th was a failure and the place did not fall until August 31st.

[4] Although the Allies suffered more killed their overall losses at Vittoria were high but not, as Rous says, as high as the French. Total Allied casualties were 33 officers and 807 men killed, 246 officers and 3,794 men wounded and 266 men missing. (Oman, *History of the Peninsular War*, Vol.VI. p.760.)

[5] Lord William Bentinck was put forward by Lord Liverpool as one of four possible candidates for the position of second-in-command of the army but was rejected by Wellington who thought him too 'despondent about the cause in the Peninsula.' (Elizabeth Longford, *Wellington; the Years of the Sword.* p.218.)

[6] Following the combats of Yecla, Biar and Castalla between Suchet and Murray the French losses were estimated at around 1,300. In his despatch to Wellington, however, Murray claimed that Suchet had lost nearly 3,000 men and that he had buried 800 French corpses. This 'most magniloquent and insincere despatch', as Oman calls it, was so absurd that Wellington - suitably unimpressed - passed it on to Lord Bathurst with the formal request that the conduct of Murray and his troops might be drawn to the attention of the Prince Regent. (Oman, *History of the Peninsular War*, Vol.VI.p.297.) (See note 6 of letter of 15.5.13)

After this place is taken Lord W. talks of marching into France which will be a fine subject for the newspaper writers, and although it will be impossible for us to make much progress in a country where the peasantry are already in arms. At the same time we may possibly advance as far as Bayonne, Pau and Tarbes to lay the most heavy contributions in all the towns and villages which will make Bonaparte very angry and it will be doing as much harm as we can without destroying the country. The idea of 100,000 men in France under a British General will make a great disturbance everywhere and we can return to the Pyrenees for the winter, which will be horrible, the whole feature of the country being always covered with snow during the six winter months. With my best love to all, believe me,

your very affectionate Son,

J.E.C. Rous.

The Convent on this side of the town was taken yesterday without much loss (about 50) the French tried to recover it but without success.[7]

---

[7] This was the Convent of St Bartholomeo which, after taking a battering from the Allied siege guns, was taken on July 17th by the 9th Regiment and three detachments of the 1st Regiment supported by some Portuguese. A French counter-attack soon afterwards was repulsed.

My Dear Mother,   Camp near Irun,
                                                September 2nd 1813.

I have been waiting some days expecting a mail from England, but I will delay no longer. You will see by the date of this letter that we have moved since I wrote last; our camp now is about one mile from Irun (spelt in the map Yrun) and about one and a half miles from Fuenterrabia, which is on the sea coast. Soult attacked us on the 31st and succeeded on our right by gaining some heights opposite our 4th and 7th Divisions, but thought it proper to retire again yesterday morning.[1] He also attacked the Spaniards in our front, just to our right of Irun. The Spaniards occupied a very strong position; for some time the conflict was doubtful. At about 4 o'clock in the evening the Spaniards succeeded in driving the French back across the Bidassoa, this they did without the assistance of British troops. They were double the number of the French, and although two of their regiments fled in all directions to the mountains upon sight of the French, altogether they have gained credit and done quite as much as we could expect of them; the French had crossed about 8,000 men on the right on the 30th and the attack commenced at daylight. Our Division is now 5,500 men; it was lucky for us that the Spaniards did not run away, otherwise it would have been necessary for us to have driven the French back again.[2]

---

[1] Following the failure of his attacks at the passes of Maya and Roncesvalles on July 25th and at Sorauren on July 28th Soult attacked again on August 31st, this time westwards across the Bidassoa River but once again he was repulsed.

[2] This was the Battle of San Marcial and it resulted in a notable success for the Spaniards under General Manuel Freire. The French attacks on the strong Spanish positions atop the ridge of San Marcial failed and although some French troops gained a foothold, prompting Freire to ask for reinforcements, the ever diplomatic Wellington, conscious of the need for a Spanish victory, declined saying, 'If I send you the English troops you ask for, they will win the battle; but as the French are already in retreat, you may as well win it for yourselves.' (Philip Henry Stanhope, *Notes of Conversations with the Duke of Wellington, 1831-1851*. London, 1888. p.22.)

While this was going on, we had detachments from the 1st, 4th and Light Divisions to assist the 5th Division in storming the town of San Sebastian, which was carried after a most severe loss on our side.[3] 400 of the 1st Division were engaged of which number 200 were Germans, 95 of the 1st Brigade and 105 of our Brigade, 50 of which were of the Coldstream. We had two officers, two sergeants and fifty men who attacked the town; one of the officers, Mr Chaplin,[4] had his thigh broken and was shot through the body; the ball has been extracted, he also had severe contusions on his head. Both the sergeants were wounded and 38 men out of 50 were either killed or wounded, - you may imagine it was pretty sharp work.[5]

Mr Chaplin had just joined us, he is son of Mr Chaplin the Member for Lincolnshire and nephew of Mrs T. Chaplin; the surgeons state him to be in the greatest possible danger, but I hope there is some chance; the 1st Brigade of Guards lost 2 officers, one was young Bridgeman,[6] a son of Lord Bradford's wounded slightly and is doing well, the other is Burrard,[7] a son of Sir Harry Burrard's, who died of his wounds yesterday; the eldest son was shot at Corunna in Sir John Moore's retreat, the second son died at sea, this was the third son. Colonel Fane who was killed at Vittoria had a brother and a nephew engaged in the storm; the former is severely wounded, the latter was killed, both fine lads between 17 and 18 years of age. Our loss in taking the town was 1,400 men;[8] we

---

[3] The storming of San Sebastian was a particularly bloody affair and as at Ciudad Rodrigo and Badajoz the victorious stormers, once inside, went berserk afterwards and sacked the town in an orgy of violence that was made worse by a fire that completely gutted the town.

[4] Ensign Thomas Chaplin survived his wounds. Gentleman Cadet from the Royal Military College. Ensign, April 4th 1811; Lieutenant, October 6th 1814; Captain, August 31st 1826.

[5] Actual Coldstream losses during the storming were 5 men killed and 1 officer and 25 men wounded with 1 missing.

[6] The Hon. Orlando Bridgeman, Ist Foot Guards. Ensign, February 14th 1811; Lieut-Capt. January 8th 1814. Went on half-pay on February 25th 1819.

[7] William Burrard, Ist Foot Guards. Ensign, January 17th 1811.

[8] The Allied loss was in fact 856 killed and 1,520 wounded.

suppose that the French who attacked the Spaniards lost about 1,000 men.[9]

I feel the loss of two shooting seasons. George Percival is gone with Mr G. Fuller to Newcastle, I do not envy him, he is a poor man and of course, right to accept a staff appointment.[10] I should like to hear of some more marriages in high life, I am afraid young men are scarce. With my kind remembrance to all at Henham,

believe me yours affectionately,

J.E.C. Rous.

---

[9] Spanish losses were 1,679. The French lost 2,500 men.

[10] Colonel Joseph Fuller had been posted to the 2nd Battalion of the Coldstream Guards on June 1st the previous year and was made a Major General on June 4th 1813. Mackinnon, (*Coldstream Guards*, p.198.) lists Percival as having left the Peninsula on March 15th to join the 2nd Battalion and I suspect that as Rous says he returned to take up an appointment on Fuller's staff.

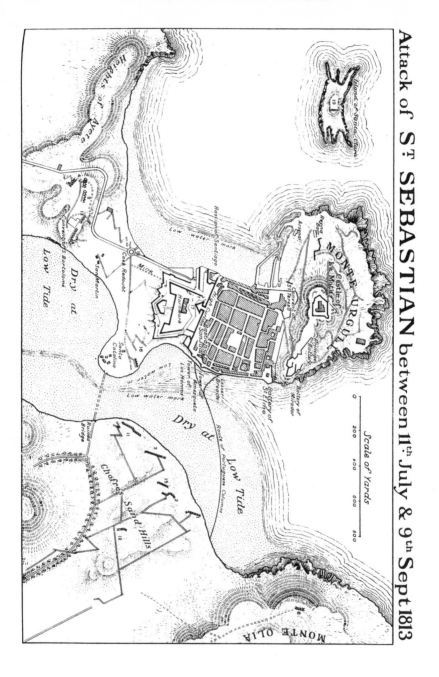

My Dear Mother,   Country house near Irun,
                                           September 17th 1813.

I have received since four letters from Henham I last wrote. Since the fall of San Sebastian we have been quite quiet; Pamplona is expected to surrender about the 30th of this month;[1] if Soult does not attack our right before that time I do not think we shall do much more this year, but retire into quarters with Pamplona and San Sebastian on our right as safeguards for the winter.[2] Lord W. Bentinck having returned to Sicily may probably be succeeded in command by Sir R. Hill, and a detachment from our army as soon as Pamplona becomes ours, to force Suchet out of Spain; this is merely my private opinion without authority.

My house here is beautifully situated with its front looking down upon the French coast. The town of Irun is seen from the right corner of my balcony, the church and some of the houses of Fuenterrabia from the left corner, the sea running into the land from the centre, and on the opposite side a French village which was formerly strongly fortified, but the works were destroyed some years ago by the French, and the fortifications of Fuenterrabia by the Spaniards at a treaty of peace. My house is about one mile from Irun, nearly the same distance from Fuenterrabia and the same from the French village (Hendaye) about half a mile from the sea. The French coast on our left is extremely fertile and nearly a flat to Bayonne opposite Irun and to the right it is more mountainous and resembles Spain for some distance. Gen. [Freire][3] is in a house immediately

---

[1] The garrison of Pamplona hung on grimly until it finally surrendered on October 31st after a blockade of some four months.

[2] Wellington, however, had other ideas and when the year of 1813 came to a close the Allied army found itself camped around the outskirts of Bayonne.

[3] General Manuel Freire (1765-1834). Victor over Reille at San Marcial, Freire had commanded in Murcia and Granada from 1810-1812 and in 1813 commanded the Army of Galicia.

opposite to mine and with a telescope I can see everybody who passes the house so distinctly as to be able to state whether he, she or they are riding or walking. We are making several small batteries about 9 or 10, on our position, which are to be filled with Spanish troops in case of attack; they are all to be made by the 1st Division.

There is very little chance of my having my promotion so soon, although I was led to believe last winter that I should be in England next June. I had bargained for a general action and the Guards to be employed, which seems very improbable just now.

I gave W. Pipe a pass to go to England about a fortnight back where I believe he is now.[4] He told me that his master, Capt. C[?] of the 18th Dragoons had returned to England, and that he had been left with his horses till they were sold; he was very smartly dressed and I hope he will turn out well. We get our newspapers pretty regularly;[5] the Muffatees will be very acceptable, they are worn in winter by a few officers, and supposed to be sent from England by the prettiest young ladies we know; I do not recommend them to soldiers, it will make them too tender, and I am convinced they would not keep them six hours; you may have the opportunity of sending me five or six pairs. My trunk is coming round from Lisbon by sea, just as I have worn out everything here. I envy William this year much, he is now enjoying the happiest time of his life. With my best love to my sisters, believe me,

Your very affectionate Son,

J.E.C. Rous.

---

[4] Pipe was Rous's former servant who had been dismissed in suspicious circumstances the previous year following the theft of some money.

[5] English newspapers were regularly sent out to the Peninsula by friends and relatives. The *Globe*, the *Morning Post*, the *Day* and the *London Chronicle* all found their way out to the army. Wellington himself took *The Times* and the *Courier*. He was, however, annoyed at the publication of many letters sent home by serving officers which betrayed important intelligence to the enemy. Indeed, it was clear that the French had benefited from such information on more than one occasion.

My Dear Mother,   Camp Near Irun,
                                    September 24th 1813.

I received yesterday your letter of the 5th inst. accompanied with the
Muffatees, and two small keys. You may depend upon my taking the
best possible care of the Muffatees, which will be of great use in the
winter, at the same time you may be assured that the soldiers will
never keep anything, that they are not absolutely obliged, nor are
they permitted on service to have anything in their possession, which
is not a regimental necessary;[1] one would be easily lost, but to
replace it would be difficult, and every soldier has a long welsh
flannel waistcoat, with sleeves, and does not suffer at all from cold
in the wrist.

    I am sorry to say that the smallest of the two keys is too large
for my red case; my old key was the most diminutive of its race, and
in these civilised days, its race is perhaps extinct. Your ague medi-
cines I have no doubt are good, here unluckily they cannot be made
up.[2] Port wine is not to be bought, and I am afraid bad Claret, Vin

---

[1] On the contrary, although the Guards regiments took pains to uphold their
dignity and appearance on campaign it was, for the majority of the army, simply
a case of 'anything goes' and dandies found themselves in their element.
Wellington's soldiers made use of all manner of items of clothing picked up after
an action or on the march and he cared little what his men wore so long as they
came into the field 'well appointed and with sixty rounds of ammunition..he never
looked to see whether their trousers were black, blue or grey...scarcely two officers
were dressed alike.' (William Grattan, *Adventures with the Connaught Rangers, 1809-
1814*. London, 1902. p.50.) Wellington himself was something of a dandy and often
wore far from regulation clothing. The subject of military dress in the Peninsula
is a study in itself.

[2] Cures for the ague were many and varied and all manner of methods were
tried by the British soldier. We find officers drinking hot spiced wine from the
saddle followed by a furious gallop, doses of quinine bark and opium, hot stones
placed on the chest and feet, water cures consisting of buckets of waters poured
over the sufferer, while the excitement of an imminent battle seems to have done
the trick for some. Joseph Donaldson, of the 94th, even swallowed a pill made
from a rolled-up spider's web! (Brett-James, *Wellington's Army*, pp.268-269.)

du Pays, Frontiniac, etc. will not answer the same purpose. We have at present three Surgeons with the regiment, all clever men, which is scarcely ever the case, and should my ague return, it would be a bad compliment to them if I was to turn Quack.[3]

We all lament the death of poor Vachell;[4] he has been in a consumption for three years, owing to the hard life he led for the first eight years he was in the Coldstream. He was one of the best feathers of the flock, and as is always the case with this regiment, the best are always killed, wounded or die a natural death. He was the eldest son of Mr. Vachell, an Essex Squire, a friend of my Fathers. The next brother is with us now, a very good sort of man, but without the vivacity and good temper of his eldest brother.

Pamplona has not fallen; there is a report that the army is to cross the Bidassoa, owing to the difficulty of communication between us and the right of our line in wet weather, this is merely a report, but I think it likely to take place when Pamplona falls, which is expected in a week or ten days; if William had gone into the 1st Guards he would have been more than half way up the list of Ensigns, with a great chance of getting several steps very soon. I can see amongst them many Officers who will not remain on service another year, all men of small fortune; unluckily our are men of no fortune and are therefore obliged to remain. Percival must be tired of living with Gen. Fuller; nothing should have induced me to have gone on his staff.[5] Pray give my kindest remembrance to all at Henham and believe me to remain. Your very affectionate Son,

J.E.C. Rous.

---

[3] The Return of Officers present with the 1st Battalion of the Coldstream in the Peninsula in 1813 shows Thomas Rose, Surgeon and William Whymper and Thomas Maynard, both as Assistant Surgeons.

[4] This was Henry W. Vachell who had been commissioned in the Coldstream as an Ensign on October 15th 1801. He died at Penzance, England, on August 29th 1813. His brother, Frederick, had joined the regiment on September 19th 1811.

[5] See note no.10 of letter dated September 2nd 1813.

My Dear Mother,   Camp near Irun,
                                                     October 6th 1813.

The good news from Germany has put the people at Bayonne in a fright;[1] a report says they are very discontented and would be happy to see the English but dread the idea of seeing the Portuguese or Spaniards, particularly the former. The French have an idea all over France that the Portuguese intend to repay them for the barbarities they committed in Portugal.[2]

Sir John Hope[3] arrived yesterday, and Sir T. Graham returns to England immediately. The Government promised to relieve him after the campaign was over, before he left England last Spring; he seems in great spirits at the idea of going home, which at the age of 65 is very natural, I must dine with him again before he leaves us, but he is four miles off, which is a long way to ride after dinner; in many points of view he is a loss to this army; we may have a better second in command, but his generosity can never be exceeded, I never saw it equalled; the attention he pays to everybody who dines with him, and his excessive good humour is remarkable at his age; his Dinner room is justly called, Liberty Hall, every person talks without reserve.[4]

---

[1] Napoleon's army had met with disaster at Grossbeeren (August 23rd), Katsbach (26th), Hagelburg (27th), Kulm (30th) and Dennewitz (September 6th).

[2] The French had more to fear from the Spaniards, the majority of whom were eventually sent home. The Portuguese, in spite of the sufferings endured by their people, were well-disciplined and made little nuisance of themselves.

[3] Lieutenant General John Hope, 4th Earl of Hopetoun (1785-1823). Commanded a division at Corunna in 1809 and at Salamanca in 1812. Commanded the left wing of the Allied army at the Nivelle and Nive but was captured during the French sortie from Bayonne in April 1814.

[4] Graham was certainly a congenial host and while at Cadiz he received a consignment of salmon and sheep from Scotland in order to entertain the Cortes and Grandees there. (Anthony Brett-James, *General Graham, Lord Lynedoch*. London, 1959. p.221.)

Hamlyn landed at Passages with three troops of the 7th Hussars about a week back,[5] I happened to ride over to Passages the very day he landed; two days afterwards I happened to ride over again and sent a mule for him and one for his bed, and sent him back the following morning with two very fine mules I bought for him cheaper and better than he could have bought himself; the detachment marched the day before yesterday on the road to Bilbao where they are to join the other half of their Regiment; he was looking very well and was in high spirits at the idea of being on service, no doubt he will soon cool.

I wish you would take every opportunity of sending me the last publications, I cannot get the Quarterly and Edinburgh reviews sent from Hatchards although I have repeatedly written about it. I want particularly two pair of short boots with buckles at the side (Kennett, 39 Silver Street, Golden Square) made some for me that I brought out and I believe has my measure, I also want about six new black neckcloths, and if you can find a key smaller than either of the last you sent and the same shape as the smallest it will be very useful. Also four Cotton night caps, I have flannel but they get hot.

There is a mail arrived at Passages, we shall not get our letters before tomorrow; Our detachment of 150 men has joined us from England which makes our battalion 900 in the country and we should fight about 750 bayonets, the 3rd Regiment have 1120 in the Country and would fight about 900 bayonets.

J.E.C. Rous.

---

[5] Lieutenant James Hamlyn, 7th Hussars.

My Dear Father,   Camp near Hendaye,
                                                   October 30th 1813.

Nothing having occurred since last week, I write merely to let you
know that I am quite well. No part of the army has moved since we
crossed the Bidassoa.[1] It has rained almost incessantly for the last
five days; the inside of my tent is nearly as wet as the outside, and
my horse and mules look terribly rough, but are not fallen away
much in flesh, which I must expect should we remain here much
longer, added to which we send seven leagues to the rear for straw,
and four leagues for corn. The price of corn is from 23 to 28 shillings
for 70 pounds, which is about four times as dear as it is in England.
During the last fortnight, our men have been sickly; we have sent
upon an average about ten men daily to our Regimental Hospital,
and till we get into houses I see no chance of that number diminish-
ing.
        We have reports that the Governor of Pamplona has offered
to give up the place upon certain terms. I cannot answer for the
truth of the report, but it seems probable, the garrison will hardly
dare to blow up the works and attempt to escape, knowing that they
are surrounded by 25,000 Spaniards who are not fond of giving
quarter.[2] Should we take up the line of the Adour for the winter, we
shall be constantly annoyed and alarmed at night by small bodies of
the French, and on the other hand if we could reach Bordeaux

---

[1] In a masterly operation Wellington's army crossed the Bidassoa River at
dawn on October 7th, his men crossing at its estuary at Irun and at Vera, some
five miles inland.

[2] The Governor of Pamplona, Cassan, had threatened to blow up the ramparts
in an attempt to secure an honourable capitulation. Wellington responded by
threatening to shoot every officer and NCO as well as a tenth of the garrison if
such a course were taken and following a breakdown in negotiations Cassan did
indeed charge his mines. When Wellington ordered an attack on the French lines
on October 30th, however, Cassan agreed to surrender. The garrison were marched
out before embarking as prisoners of war for England.

(which is out of the question) I am convinced that the Spaniards would murder every man, woman or child they met without exception; could we put sufficient confidence in the Spaniards to give them up our present position which is very strong, and retire ourselves about six leagues to the rear for three months, it would save the lives of many soldiers who will die in the winter if we remain here much longer. Soult has, I am told, put three Generals under arrest for giving up this position so easily on the 7th inst, and calls the two Divisions who were engaged the two worst in his army. He was at Bayonne when he heard of the attack, and before he reached his Divisions, heard that the British troops had carried the position with a slight loss; he is an extremely passionate man, and hated by his men, more particularly by his Officers, but is I believe the best General in the French army.[3] The Moniteur states that Bonaparte was at Dresden on the 7th, but I trust he has given up the line of the Elbe before this time or been well beaten.[4]

I shall never mention the word Promotion, it is quite at an end. Hotham[5] who was returned slightly wounded at Salamanca turns out to be severely wounded; the Surgeons say that the hip bone was touched, and a piece must come away before the wound can heal, I shall advise him to go home. With my love to all,

J.E.C. Rous.

---

[3] Soult was absent from the area of the main crossing at the estuary of the Bidassoa as he considered this virtually impassable. Unfortunately for him this was exactly where Wellington decided to cross. Soult subsequently blamed both Reille and Maucune for the ease at which the Allies were able to cross the Bidassoa but although Reille could not be held responsible - he had too few troops to cover his own sector - Maucune certainly was guilty of negligence. British troops had crossed in broad daylight and yet the French defenders did not fire a shot until many of them were safely across. (Sir Peter Hayman, *Soult, Napoleon's Maligned Marshal,* London, 1990. p.197.)

[4] The *Moniteur* was the mouthpiece of Napoleon's France. It obviously did not carry news of Napoleon's crushing defeat at Leipzig on October 16th-19th.

[5] Ensign Beaumont Hotham, afterwards Lord Hotham. Gentleman Cadet from the Royal Military College. Commissioned as Ensign on June 27th 1810.

THE PASSAGE OF THE BIDASSOA
October 7th 1813

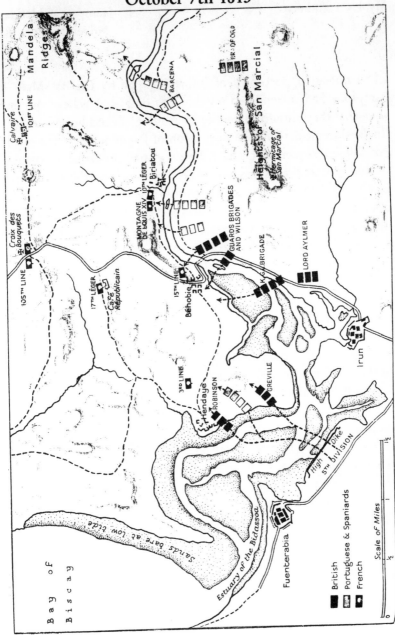

My Dear Father,   Camp near Hendaye,
                                                   November 5th 1813.

I had not an opportunity of informing you by the last Mail that
Pamplona had surrendered on the 30th or 31st; I believe the terms
were that they should surrender to the English and be embarked for
England immediately. The possession of Pamplona is of the greatest
possible consequence to the Allies; we shall immediately throw in
twelve months provisions, and it becomes a safe barrier for our right
and San Sebastian for our left, should we ever be driven back by
double our numbers. I defy anything less than double to move us
one step from our present position. The Second Division has been
obliged to retire a little, because the roads were so bad that the
Commissariat Department could not furnish them with Rum and
Biscuit. We have a great many men employed making roads; as soon
as they are finished we shall attack the French position or rather turn
their left and force them to retire. I will endeavour to give you an
idea of their position. I have no doubt that you will make out this
writing with the assistance of my Mother; pray do not show it out
of the Family it is such a scrawl.

It has rained constantly for nearly a fortnight; the inside of
my tent was nearly as wet as the outside. We have now fine frosty
weather which seems inclined to last for some time. Letters are not
received at the Orderly Room as they used to be; they are either
opened and sent back, or sent to Greenwood and there is a chance
that we never may receive them; perhaps you know the Adjutant
General to the Forces, letters directed to him neither pay Land Nor
Sea Carriage. With my kindest remembrance to all, believe me
Your very affectionate Son,

J.E.C. Rous.

My Dear Mother,   Camp one league in front of
                                                    St Jean de Luz.
                                              November 14th 1813.

We attacked the enemy's position on the other side of the Nivelle
with great success on the morning of the 10th inst.[1] We commenced
on the left by taking their most advanced Breast Work without loss,
and the picquets kept up a fire from the left to the right of out line.
Lord W. then attacked the enemy with the Light, 4th and 7th
Divisions and a large force of Spaniards, and Sir Rowland Hill with
the 2nd, 3rd and 6th Divisions attempted to turn their left flank.
Near the middle of the day we had succeeded in every point and
Soult who had been the whole day at St Jean de Luz, fancying that
the real attack was on his right, did not receive the intelligence of
our attack till between one and two o'clock after the whole was over.
He then gave his orders for retreat and the whole French army
marched at sunset for the vicinity of Bayonne. On the morning of
the 11th we crossed the Nivelle [and] marched through St Jean de
Luz to a small village called Guetarie.

        We are now in camp about one mile from it; the French lost
800 prisoners and 45 pieces of cannon. I suppose our loss will be
2500, that of the French about the same.[2] In the left column light
troops were chiefly engaged; Anstruther[3] is wounded in the calf of

---

[1] This was the Battle of the Nivelle, fought on November 10th. As at the
crossing of the Bidassoa Soult was again fooled by Wellington as to the main point
of attack. Soult had expected an attack along the coast but instead Wellington
chose to attack the weaker French defences that centred around the Lesser Rhune,
a large hill that dominated the area.

[2] Total Allied losses were 32 officers and 372 men killed, 145 officers and 1,903
men wounded. 4 officers and 69 men were listed as missing; a total of 2,526.
French losses were 37 officers and 414 men killed, 113 officers and 2,524 men
wounded with 34 officers and 1,199 men missing; a total of 4,321.

[3] Ensign William Anstruther. Commissioned as Ensign on July 5th 1810;
Lieutenant, March 17th 1814. Retired February 26th 1817.

his leg, we do not know whether severely or slightly. The cavalry are coming up by forced marches; when they arrive we shall cross the Nive and then the Adour. In case his Lordship should like to see Bordeaux this year, cavalry will be of great use - the country from Bayonne to Bordeaux is the most barren open and flat part of France, [and] Bayonne is not very strong, at least there are hills on this side of it which command the town, and I trust we shall burn it in case they refuse to surrender; we must not stop at trifles in an enemy's country.[4] They say Bonaparte is at Paris and is expected here. I hope he will come; the English will fight with double vigour against any army commanded by Napoleon le Grand. I hope never to see Spain or Portugal [again as] we are now in a civilized country. The news (from) the north is glorious; the Moniteur confesses the loss [of a] Corps which they call 12,000 men, but must be at least 30,000 ; they attribute it to having blown up the bridge across the Snale (I think is the name) without knowing that these troops were on the other side, but the good people of Paris will never believe such nonsense;[5] the truth is they were fairly outmanoeuvred and cut off by the Allies, and Bonaparte has proved to all the world that he is no general when opposed to equally good troops whose chiefs are not to be bribed. He has called conscription for 1814 and 1815 which I hope will cause general dissatisfaction.[6] We may now hope for peace,

---

[4] On the contrary, Wellington's policy was exactly the opposite. He was only too aware of the dangers of inflaming local feelings against the Allies. The French experience in Spain at the hands of the guerrillas was a painful and expensive one and the last thing he needed was the emergence of a similar resistance movement in France. It was vital that therefore that discipline was maintained amongst his men, hence the removal of the majority of the Spanish troops once across the French border.

[5] The river was, in fact, the River Elster. Around 20,000 men were lost on October 18th when a bridge across the river was blown up prematurely by the retreating French, leaving their rearguard stranded on the wrong side of the river. Both General Lauriston and General Reynier were captured whilst the wounded Marshal Poniatowski drowned while trying to swim across.

[6] Around 936,000 conscripts and discharged reservists were called up in the winter of 1813-14 including 150,000 men not due for service until 1815. (Philip Haythornthwaite, *Napoleon's Military Machine*, Tunbridge Wells, 1988. p.148.)

the treachery of the Saxons and Bavarians must have been mortifying to the French.[7]

It has rained incessantly here for three days and I have been wet all day and have turned into a wet bed every night; there is no remedy. I am now suffering from cold and rheumatism which I fear will tell much against me some years hence, there is only one consolation, that the French are as wet as we are. With my best love,

Your very affectionate Son,

J.E.C. Rous.

Lord W. has ordered the army of Galicia under Gen. Giron to the rear for plundering instead of fighting.[8]

---

[7] The Saxons and Bavarians had changed sides during the 1813 German campaign - the Saxons actually deserted the French cause during the Battle of Leipzig on October 16th-19th 1813.

[8] Giron's brigades were sent back across the Pyrenees to the villages of the Basque country Wellington wrote one of his more caustic letters to the Spanish general, Freire, 'Indiscipline is general in your corps....Now I do not enter France in order to plunder: I have not had so many thousands of officers and men killed and wounded merely in order that the survivors should be able to rob the French. On the contrary, it is my duty, and the duty of all of us, to stop pillage, especially if we intend to make our army live off the resources of the country.' (*Wellington's Dispatches*, Vol.XI. pp.288-289.)

THE BATTLE OF THE NIVELLE
November 10th 1813

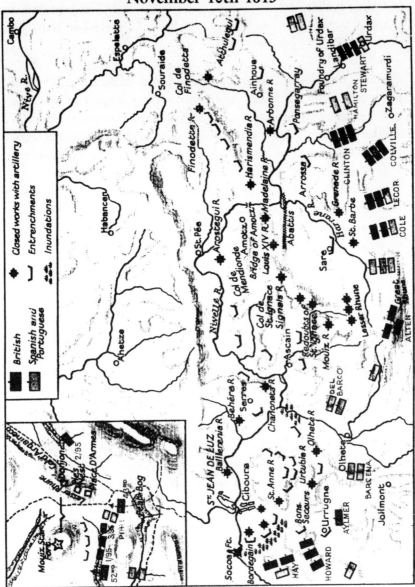

My Dear Father,   St Jean de Luz,
                                                       November 27th 1813.

The two Brigades of Guards have been cantoned here since the 19th,
the whole army are under cover within three leagues of this place,
and the Spaniards have recrossed the Bidassoa for winter quarters. We
are daily receiving drafts from England; should the Spaniards recruit
as they ought to, we shall endeavour to take some impression in
France during the Spring; we know that the Austrian advance is at
Padua, and their main body at Gerona; in a few months Italy will be
free. On the other hand we hear that the Crown Prince is moving
off towards Holland;[1] Bonaparte has demanded 300,000 men, 150,000
of which are to be ready in six weeks, or at least the Senate has
granted that number, we hear that his demands were much greater.
     Lord W. will have a disposable force of 200,000 men.
including cavalry by the 1st of next February, and if any fortified
towns in the rear of our Catalonian army should fall into our hands
during the winter, which we have every reason to suppose that some
must for want of provisions, Suchet in that case must retire into
France. The last Moniteur is the only French paper for some weeks
that has not abused the English, which looks as if Bonaparte was
inclined to ask for Peace. The inhabitants of this town like the
English very much; we received last week 500 women from Bayonne;
Headquarters being in the town makes it very pleasant, besides which
we have plenty of merchant vessels from England with Claret and
Champagne.[2] If you know of any person wishing to make 5 or £600,

---

[1] Following the Allies' victory at Leipzig their armies began to converge on
France in a three-pronged attack. While 60,000 men under the Crown Prince
Bernadotte were moving into Holland, Schwartzenberg's 210,000 Austrians
advanced from the Upper Rhine and Marshal Blucher's 70,000 Prussians from the
Lorraine. Another Austrian army under Bellegarde, were advancing through Italy.

[2] After years of having to supply his army from Lisbon Wellington, was now
able to secure supplies by using the ports of northern Spain, such as Pasajes.

he can do it by bringing out a cargo of wax and tallow candles; we pay 8d for wax per lb. and 4d for tallow candles at present. Pray write me word upon what system the volunteering for the Militia for service is;[3] the Prince's Speech at the opening of Parliament was as much to the purpose as possible, I should think it was too good a production to be Lord Liverpool;[4] Lord Grenville's[5] recantation must have been most pleasing to our Ministry, if Perceval or Pitt had been alive now, they would almost have died for joy at the present state of affairs.[6] I forgot to mention in my last letter that we had a man desert to the enemy, it is the only instance in our Brigade during the five years we have been on service. The unlucky part of the story is that the rascal miraculously escaped dying of the Fever we had last year at Mongualde. Pray direct to me in France instead of Spain in future, I trust never to see that horrible country again. With my best love to all, Your affectionate Son,

J.E.C. Rous.

---

[3] The Militia had become a contentious issue at this time. Wellington was fighting hard to retain his 'Provisional Battalions' - battalions made up of veterans from units weakened either by action or sickness which, rather than send home to recruit, as should have been the case, he chose to keep as they were experienced campaigners. However, the Minister of War, Lord Bathurst, recommended replacing these with Militia battalions, a move that Wellington was opposed to on the grounds that they lacked all usefulness and discipline. He suggested that the Militia be used only for drafts for front-line regiments. Despite a bounty of £5 for every NCO and private only a single Militia brigade of 2,800 men could be induced for service in the Peninsula and that arrived too late to take part in any action. (Oman, *History of the Peninsular War*, Vol.VII. pp.148-149 and J.W. Fortescue, *A History of the British Army*, London, 1920. Vol.IX, pp.416-420.)

[4] R.B. Jenkinson, 2nd Earl of Liverpool (1770-1828). Became Prime Minister, June 1812.

[5] William Wyndham, 1st Baron Grenville (1759-1834). A supporter of the war against Napoleon.

[6] Spencer Perceval (1762-1812). Prime Minister in 1809, he was assassinated in the lobby of the House of Commons in 1812. William Pitt, (1759-1806). Prime Minister 1804-06. Both were committed to the policy of war with France.

THE BATTLE OF THE NIVE
December 10th 1813

1814 - ADVANCE TO VICTORY

In the face of extreme pressure from the Austrian, Russian and Prussian armies Napoleon withdrew some 10,000 valuable men from Soult in January 1814, thus weakening further the force barring Wellington's advance into France. And Manpower was not the only problem facing the over-stretched French as supplies, arms and ammunition were diverted for use elsewhere. Wellington's own men, on the other hand, enjoyed regular quantities of clothing, food, arms and ammunition which were supplied to them by the Royal Navy through the ports of northern Spain and southern France. With events turning against him it was only a matter of time before the final defeat of Napoleon, even though his 1814 campaign in France has often been called his most brilliant as he raced from one crisis point to the next, winning several victories as he did so. But the odds were too great even for him as the Allied armies of Prussia, Russia and Austria bore down on Paris from the north and east. But for Wellington's army there were still some obstacles to be overcome and some hard fighting ahead before the inevitable.

On February 23rd British troops, under General Hope, crossed the Adour, west of Bayonne. The operation was a hazardous one, British troops crossing the river on pontoon rafts which could only be worked during slack tide. In the evening, two light companies of the Coldstream and four battalion companies of the 3rd Guards made the crossing and held off two large columns of enemy infantry with the assistance of artillery and a discharge of the new Congreve rockets which scattered the startled French. The next day saw Wellington's force firmly established on the opposite bank of river and by February 26th a bridge of boats had been constructed for regular use.

On February 27th the Battle of Orthes was fought, as a result of which Soult was forced to fall back towards Toulouse, which he entered on March 24th. On March 30th the Russians and Prussians entered Paris and on April 4th Napoleon abdicated. Unfortunately, the news did not reach either Wellington or Soult until the 12th, by which time a major engagement had been fought, namely the Allied assault on Toulouse. Wellington sustained 4,568 casualties in a bitter, confused assault which need never have happened.

Wellington entered Toulouse on the 12th but there was still a tragic and bloody postscript to come, for on April 14th, whether out of sheer anger or simply ignorant of the armistice, General Thouvenot, the governor of Bayonne, launched a sortie, centred against the 2nd Brigade of Guards at St Etienne. The officer in charge, Major General Hay, was killed almost immediately and the French took possession of the village. The French were eventually driven back but not before inflicting heavy casualties on the British including the capture of General Hope during the fight. This pointless exercise cost the Allies and French some 1,743 casualties between them. Bayonne continued to hold out until April 26th but the Peninsular War effectively ended on April 17th when Soult surrendered to Wellington.

Six years of war had finally come to an end and although it would need one final, momentous effort one year later at Waterloo to defeat Napoleon for ever, the fighting was over for Wellington's Peninsular army. As the war drew towards its inevitable conclusion some regiments, including a number of companies of the Guards, were sent to Holland to take part in the campaign in the Low Countries under Sir Thomas Graham, while even more were despatched to North America where the war against the United States had been raging since 1812. Many units that had marched to glory in Portugal and Spain were subsequently destroyed in the disastrous and ill-fated - not to mention unnecessary - attack on Andrew Jackson's troops at Chalmette Field, New Orleans, in January 1815, during which Edward Pakenham, Wellington's brother-in-law, was killed.

When Napoleon escaped from Elba in February 1815, British troops hurried back from America to join their old commander but many of them arrived just too late to share in the glory of June 18th

1815 at Waterloo. On that fateful day his 'infamous' army, as Wellington himself called it, was a mixture of British, Dutch, Belgians and Brunswickers, to name but a few of the contingents that fought under him that day. It was a pale shadow of that which had marched, it is calculated, over 6,000 miles and had fought undefeated across the Iberian Peninsula, an army of which Wellington later said he could have anywhere and done anything with, it was in such perfect order. And as John Rous himself recalled, when he spoke to Wellington on the subject many years later, the Duke said that had he had with him his old Peninsular army the Battle of Waterloo would have been over in half an hour.

My Dear Father,   Camp before St Esprit,
                                             February 27th 1814.

The 1st Division crossed the Adour on the days of the 23rd and 24th
without any further loss than seven men wounded which were of our
Brigade. The French attacked with 1200 men about five o'clock on
the evening of the 23rd, at which time we had only 500 men of our
Brigade on this side of the river, and a few men with rockets. They
drove in our advanced posts and were moving rapidly upon the main
body. When they were within 200 yards we fired a few rockets at
them which frightened them so much that they immediately retired
in confusion. Our light companies pursued them, and killed some;
we took four prisoners, none of whom had been soldiers more than
two months. Had they advanced 100 yards nearer, very few would
have returned to Bayonne; the French Officers were seen beating
their men to get them on, but the unsteady behaviour of the
conscripts was worse than anything I ever saw, excepting the usual
behaviour of the Spaniards, and they could not have done worse;
1200 British under the same circumstances would have cut to pieces
every man; we had no retreat, the sea on our left and our rear and
the Adour on our right, everything depended upon the steady
conduct of our men, which could not be exceeded.[1] We now have
here the 1st Division, two Portuguese Brigades, two regiments of

---

[1] The crossing of the river Adour on February 23rd-24th was a bold operation,
fraught with danger, but one which proved a complete success. Rous's account of
the crossing by the Guards is very accurate. With only two companies of the
Coldstream and four of the 3rd Guards across they were attacked by around 1,000
French troops. However, the Guards, commanded by Major General Stopford,
were 'judiciously posted' amidst some sand hills and checked the enemy's advance
with some accurate musketry. Most agree that the fight was settled by a discharge
of Congreve rockets, a new weapon as yet rarely encountered by the French. The
rockets exploded at the head of the French column, throwing them back towards
Bayonne in disorder. (Mackinnon, *Coldstream Guards*, Vol.II. p.200, and Oman, *A
History of the Peninsular War*, Vol.VII. pp.334-336.)

John Edward Cornwallis Rous, later 2nd Earl of Stradbroke,
in the uniform of the Coldstream Guards.

The Battle of Salamanca. Fought on July 22nd 1812,
it was John Rous' baptism of fire.

Wellington and his staff at the Battle of the Nivelle.

The Guards enter France, October 1813.

The bridge of boats across the Adour.

Irun, on the Spanish-French border.

The Sortie from Bayonne on April 14th 1814.

The portable
Aneroid
Barometer used
by William
Rufus Rous
during his
military career.
Commissioned
as ensign in the
Coldstream on
December 7th
1812, he was
John Rous'
younger brother
and is mentioned
in the letters.

The Gorget and
Coldstream Stars
worn by John Rous
during Wellington's
campaigns.

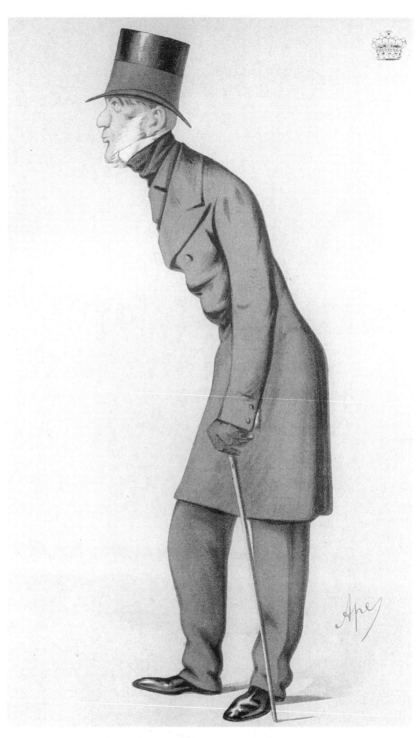

A Spy cartoon of the Earl of Stradbroke,
published by *Vanity Fair* on July 31st 1875.

The Earl of
Stradbroke, as
John Rous
became
in 1827.

Henham Hall
in Suffolk.

A family tradition - the profession of arms. John Rous' son George, 3rd Earl of Stradbroke (seated); and grandsons, (standing from left) John, 4th Earl and Keith, 5th Earl, both Royal Navy; Peter, 16th/5th The Queen's Royal Lancers; and George, The Life Guards.

Lieutenant General the Honourable Sir William Rous KCB OBE and Lady Rous with their sons James (right), who has recently joined the Coldstream Guards and is at Oxford University, and Richard (left), who is at Harrow School. 10th March 1992

cavalry, [and] 4000 Spaniards. The bridge is to be finished tomorrow night,[2] after which we may expect our baggage. We have been five nights without tents but luckily it has not rained the whole time. The inhabitants do not mind us in the least; they farm, and the women and children sit at home in the most perfect ease, selling their fowls at 5s. each. They all appear to dislike the French because they never pay for anything.[3] Lord W. has crossed the Gave d'Oloron and was to be near Paux yesterday; they say that Soult is retiring upon the interior leaving Bordeaux open.[4] The inhabitants say that we might take possession of the bridge at Dax if we choose to move forward directly. We hear that the French have from 4 to 12,000 men in Bayonne, I should think 4,000 men nearer the mark.[5] The right of the army are living in all sorts of luxury. There is a report that the effective part of the army in Holland is to join us; they appear to be of no use where they are now, whereas our being able to advance into the heart of France would be the last blow, and must settle the thing.[6] I have no time to write more. Your very affectionate Son,

J.E.C. Rous.

---

[2] The river had originally been crossed by means of pontoon rafts. Once across the river, however, the pontoons were substituted for boats and by the evening of February 26th a bridge of boats had been completed across the estuary of the Adour a little below Bayonne.

[3] Wellington did his utmost to ensure that provisions were paid for by his army unlike the French who were notorious for their practice of living off the land, even when in their own country. It was a distinction that Wellington was keen to uphold in order to gain the confidence of the French people.

[4] The very day, in fact, that Rous wrote this letter Wellington fought the Battle of Orthes which resulted in Soult's retirement towards Toulouse. It was Hill's corps that crossed the Gave d'Oloron on the 23rd.

[5] The French garrison in Bayonne actually numbered around 11,000. (Fortescue, *History of the Army*, Vol.IX. p.500.)

[6] On November 24th 1813, six companies of the Coldstream Guards had sailed to Holland as part of a force of some 4,000 men under Sir Thomas Graham which was to take part in an attack on the Dutch town of Bergen-op-Zoom.

My Dear Mother,   Camp before St Esprit,
                                              near Bayonne,
                                            March 13th 1814.

Bad fortune remains always with the 1st Division; we are now left
here with the 5th Division, two Portuguese Brigades and one English
to undertake the siege of Bayonne, unless an armistice should prevent
us, or some probability of an immediate peace. The garrison consists
of 4,000 old troops and 7,000 young troops, they have at least nine
months' provisions, perhaps more. The besieging army at present is
only 10,000 men and the number to be besieged is 11,000 which
appears absurd. The usual calculation is, that besiegers should be
double the number of the besieged;[1] under the present circumstances,
should we lose many men before there is a practicable breach made,
we must receive another Division before we can storm the town;
there are great speculations whether we shall ever commence a siege
or not. There are 160 pieces of heavy artillery at Passages, at present
there are no means of conveying them; they must be brought up by
land, and if you average 14 horses to each gun, you may judge that
the number required will be very great, besides which we shall
require 200 cars to bring shot, shells &c. The difficulties are great,
but his Lordship has made up his mind, and if we hear nothing to
the contrary we shall commence operations in a fortnight.

     At present we cool our heels one day and night out of every
four in a lane watching their batteries in case they may like to attack
us, which is particularly pleasant,[2] as it has rained or snowed nearly

---

[1] This calculation is based on the fact that a besieging force needed to be strong
enough not only to keep a town or city properly surrounded by also to keep at
bay any relieving force that might interfere with the siege operations.

[2] The complicated business of siege warfare required the besiegers to be ultra
vigilant lest the beleaguered army launch a sortie which not only caused casualties
but would cost the Allies hundreds of valuable siege tools which Wellington's
poorly-equipped army could ill-afford to lose as was the case at Badajoz in 1812.

every day for the last month. The other days I have been in camp, till yesterday, when General Stopford[3] kindly gave me up a room in his house for myself and another for my baggage and to cook in. We are kept in perfect ignorance respecting the rest of the army; we know that Marshal Beresford[4] has left Mont Marsan on the road to Bordeaux; where Lord W. is we know not. Suchet has joined Soult with 9,000 men; we understand that the Marquis intends to attack him the first opportunity; the first particulars I shall hear respecting the last action will be in the Times or Morning Post. I am very sorry for Lord March who is I fear dangerously wounded.[5] He dined with me [the letter is torn away here]

We have received papers to the 15th of February only, although there are English papers at St Jean de Luz up to the 2nd of March. Our letters are travelling about France. I dined with an aide-de-camp of Genl. Beresford's yesterday who is just arrived from Lisbon, and saw there 10,000 Portuguese troops waiting for transports to convey them to Passages; our reinforcements from England are not arrived.

[the letter is again torn here] armistice to give time for the Crown Prince, and the Austrian army in Italy to join, and then refuse to make peace with Bonaparte upon any terms unless he agrees to abdicate the Throne; the principle is bad, but it is what Bonaparte would do, was he in the situation of the Allies. If William has not left England before you receive this, pray desire him to bring for me a new cap from Cater's,[6] plain [black] cloth with a round peak, a

---

[3] Major General the Hon. E. Stopford, 3rd Foot Guards. Commanded the 2nd Brigade of Guards, 1st Division in the Peninsula.

[4] Viscount William Beresford (1768-1854). Saw much service overseas and led the ill-fated expedition to the Rio de la Plata in 1806. His main achievement in the Peninsula was the training of the Portuguese army, in which he was created a Marshal. He commanded the Allied army at Albuera in 1811 but was criticised for his handling of the battle badly in spite of his eventual narrow victory.

[5] Captain Charles Lennox, Earl of March (1791-1860). Eldest son of the Duke of Richmond - who gave the Waterloo Ball - he was ADC to Wellington throughout most of the Peninsular War. He was badly wounded at Orthes.

[6] Cater's milliners.

gold band round the cap; mine is completely worn out, and Cater will trust me till I return to England.[7] With my best love to all at Henham. Believe me,

Your very affectionate Son,

J.E.C. Rous.

---

[7] As with the rest of the uniform, the headdress also suffered from the wear and tear of campaign and from the elements. When the Peninsular War began British officers had worn the old cocked hat, worn 'fore and aft', but from 1812 they adopted the new-style 'Belgic' shako, a cylindrical shape with a false front, which was worn by other ranks also. An oilskin cover was provided to protect the shako in wet weather but in the event of a soaking it needed only a spell of hot weather afterwards to distort its shape and make it almost unwearable.

THE COUNTRY BETWEEN
BAYONNE AND PAMPLONA

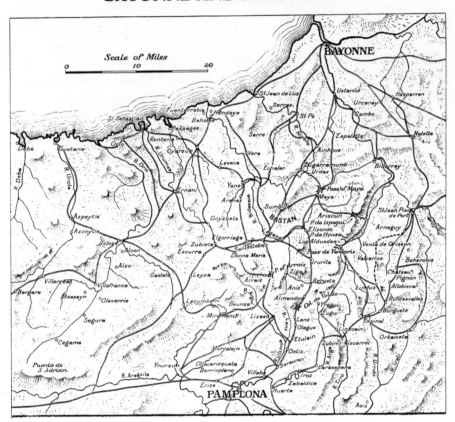

My Dear Mother,   On picquet at St Etienne,
                                              March 18th 1814.

Appearances have been so good lately, that I must write to you.
Although I cannot get your letters, the last I received from you was
dated February 20th, there has been a Mail at San Sebastian up to the
3rd of March for several days. Unluckily for us, our Post Master is
a clever fellow, and amuses himself with constructing bridges instead
of attending to his office.[1] The consequence is that our letters come
in a bullock car from San Sebastian, and take six days to perform a
journey which mules would do in one.

    You will be glad to hear that our 4th and 7th Divisions are
at Bordeaux with Marshal Beresford and 2 Brigades of light cavalry,
the 12th and 16th, 13th and 14th [Light] Dragoons. Colonel Vivian[2]
who commands the last mentioned Brigade was sent forward to
inform the Mayor that the English were about to enter the town as
friends and that private property &c. should be preserved; upon
which the Mayor with the two principle inhabitants went out to
meet our Marshal, and re-entered the town with white cockades in
their hats;[3] the white flag was hoisted all over the town and every-

---

[1] This was Lieutenant Colonel Richard Sturgeon (1781-1814), of the Royal Staff
Corps. Sturgeon had constructed the temporary bridge at Alcantra and the bridge
of boats over the Adour. In April 1813 he had been placed in charge of the Post
Office but incurred Wellington's wrath when the service became disorganised
following the Battle of Orthes. Either through remorse or because his pride had
been hurt, he deliberately got himself killed at the outposts at Vic-en-Bigorre on
March 19th 1814. (S.G.P. Ward, *Wellington's Headquarters*, London, 1957. p.191.
and Jock Haswell, *The First Respectable Spy; The Life and Times of Colquhoun Grant,
Wellington's Head of Intelligence*. London, 1969. p.208.)

[2] Richard Hussey Vivian, 1st Baron Vivian. Took over command of Grant's
cavalry brigade on November 24th 1813.

[3] The white cockade was the badge worn by royalist supporters. When the
Mayor of Bordeaux, Jean-Baptiste Lynch, entered the town with Beresford, he tore
the Legion of Honour from his coat and fixed the white cockade in his hat, thus
precipitating an outbreak of royalist fervour as thousands followed suit.

body was considered as an enemy to the cause, that did not appear with white cockades. The people were informed that the Royal Duke would arrive in half an hour; loud cries of 'Vive le Roi' echoed from every street, and divine service was immediately performed, after which they proclaimed the Duke as their Prince.[4]

I have seen the Bordeaux Gazette which speaks of the English in the most enthusiastic manner; we expect the same thing will spread for miles. The people have offered to raise 10,000 men, after this time, should we make peace with Bonaparte. I shall pity the unfortunate inhabitants who must suffer for their loyalty when the third largest town in France begins; we may hope that they will be well supported.[5]

The garrison of Bayonne is ascertained correctly, 4,000 old soldiers, 7,000 conscripts, and 4,000 sick which were nearly all the sick of Soult's army, and we think they cannot have more than three month's provisions, which is an enormous store for 15,000 men. Fancy our misery when we know that the Guards would have been the first troops to have entered Bordeaux had it not been for this place; Balls and Dinners, Operas &c. every night, instead of picquets one night out of three and fatigue parties of sometimes ten hours almost every day, which will probably end in a siege. I understand that Lord W. is at [Mirande ?] and Soult between that place and Toulouse.

A messenger passed us yesterday who left London on the 11th; he says that our drafts marched from London on the 28th, I hear my brother started with them. There is no chance of Hotham going out of the Coldstream while peace appears probable.[6] We have

---

[4] The duke in question was Louis Antoine, Duke d'Angoulême (1775-1844). He was the elder son of the Comte d'Artois and later became Charles X of France.

[5] The Duke d'Angoulême had offered to raise a Royalist army to fight for the restoration of the Bourbons. Wellington had no objection but insisted that the Duke himself would have to raise the money to pay for it. As it turned out, there was little support for such a move. There were plenty of officers but no rank and file. (Oman, *History of the Peninsular War*, Vol.VII. pp.398-399.)

[6] Ensign Beaumont Hotham was due to inherit his title as Lord Hotham.

not had any confirmation of the report that the Crown Prince had beaten Bonaparte under the walls of Paris, and taken a general and several prisoners, also that the National Guard refused to march out of Paris. All this is believed.[7] I kept your Birthday yesterday, and drank your health in a glass of Burgundy. With my best love to all at Henham, believe me,

Your very affectionate Son,

J.E.C. Rous.

---

[7] This was not true, however. Napoleon's 1814 campaign in France has often been called his greatest. In spite of the tremendous odds stacked against him Napoleon fought a tireless campaign to drive the Allies from 'the sacred soil'. As late as March 13th he defeated the Allies at Rheims.

March 19th 1814.

Two mails are just arrived here bringing letters up to the 8th. I have received letters from Henham of the 5th and 6th. We are more sanguine than you respecting the Allies; Bonaparte acting from a centre can always bring a larger body upon one point than the Allies can have to oppose him, although he is actually inferior in numbers to the Allied army, but in advancing he naturally risks having his flank closed upon, the consequence of which would be the loss of many prisoners. Blucher's troops appear to have behaved like heroes, I wish he had the entire command.[1] The system for the Allies is to fight whenever they can upon fair ground which will bring the thing to a certainty. Supposing one side to be 300,000 and the other 200,000, supposing each to lose 150,000 men the Allies will then have 150,000 men against 50,000, although the French army will (I am convinced) refuse to fight before they lose 40,000 men more and somebody will have spirit enough to kill Bonaparte. The people here have been so much deceived about Bonaparte's victories, that they would not believe it if he was to gain a considerable advantage. I expect William every day. Adieu. The 4th Division are recalled from Bordeaux; we expect to hear of a battle between Soult and Lord W. you need not fear the event.[2]

---

[1] Gerhard Leberecht, Count Blücher, Prince of Wahlstadt (1742-1819). During the 1814 campaign Blücher's Prussians had defeated the French at La Rothiere (February 1st) and Laon (March 9th). Sandwiched between these victories, however, were defeats suffered at Brienne (January 29th), Champaubert (February 10th), Montmirail (11th), Château-Thierry (12th), Vauchamps (14th) and Craonne (March 7th). Blücher was again defeated by Napoleon at Ligny on June 16th 1815, during the Waterloo campaign - where he was ridden over by French cavalry - but returned two days later to decide the day at Waterloo.

[2] Rous is probably referring to the Battle of Orthes, fought on February 27th, of which, in spite of his close proximity to the area, he had still heard nothing.

March 20th.

I have opened this letter again to say that I have received a letter from Colonel Brand[3] to say, that if I intend to purchase my Lieutenancy the regulation which is £600 should be placed in the Agent's hands immediately.[4] Hotham has succeeded to his title and estate, I shall see him today to know how soon he intends to quit.[5] Soult has again retired.

Yours, &c.

J.E.C. Rous.

---

[3] The Hon. Henry Brand. Commissioned as Ensign, Coldstream Guards on April 27th 1793; Lieutenant, June 23rd 1795; Captain, October 25th 1806; officially became Lieutenant-Colonel on July 25th 1814. Major-General, July 19th 1821.

[4] This is rather curious since the regulation fee for a Lieutenancy in the Guards was, in fact, £1,500 compared to £550 for the similar in an ordinary Line regiment. (P. Haythornthwaite, *Wellington's Military Machine*, Tunbridge Wells, 1989. p.26.)

[5] Beaumont Hotham, who joined the Coldstream the day before Rous, left the Peninsula to assume his title as Lord Hotham. However, he did not leave the regiment and later fought at Waterloo as Captain, 6th Company, and is pictured in the painting of the Waterloo Banquet at Apsley House. He eventually reached the rank of Lieutenant-Colonel.

THE COUNTRY BETWEEN
BAYONNE AND ORTHEZ

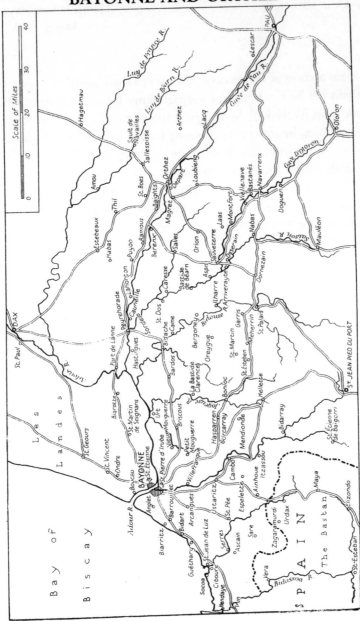

My Dear Father,   Camp before Bayonne,
                                  March 27th 1814.

William arrived at Passages on the 20th; I only heard of it yesterday. He tells me he has bought a baggage pony for eight dollars, which I think most likely will die before it arrives here. I have sent my mules to assist him, he starts this morning from Laso, and will be at St Jean de Luz tomorrow. We have done nothing here, but continue the blockade under fire. There has been constant wet weather and the men look very ill. Lord W. is supposed to be near Toulouse. There is a report that the Allies are in Paris, but the authority is bad.[1] We have nothing from England of later date than when I wrote last. With all my best love to all. Believe me,

Your very affectionate Son,

J.E.C. Rous.

---

[1] The Allies did not enter Paris until March 31st.

My Dear Mother,   Camp before Bayonne,
                                                        April 9th 1814.

I write every week, although it is impossible for me to give you any
news, we are kept in perfect ignorance respecting the rest of the
army, and do not yet know the particulars of the action which took
place on the 27th of February;[1] we hear that Sir Rowland Hill
crossed the Garonne on the 31st, but was obliged to recross on the
1st on account of the badness of the roads;[2] ere this the whole army
are on the other side no doubt. Soult is supposed to be weak, and
not inclined to fight, whereas our victorious army can march
wherever they like. It puts us out of spirits to fancy our situation
and that of the rest of the army; we are taking the most unpleasant
of all duties, they are living in luxury, and beholding one of the most
beautiful Countries in Europe;
        Toulouse is an excellent town, and the scenery round it is a
perfect garden. The inhabitants are civil, and they are glad to have
the English in their houses; there are Balls &c. in all the large towns
the army passes through, and since the Guards are supposed to carry
with them all the gold of the army, we should be more happy even
than we should be in England. Here we see nobody, nothing going
on, not even a library within reach; when we are not on duty the
only amusement is to see the trees and grass grow, it puts me in

---

[1] It is quite surprising that Rous had yet to hear the details of the Battle of
Orthes, fought almost six weeks before on February 27th. News and information
flowed freely in the army and a major engagement would have been a leading
subject for discussion. Although the Coldstream Guards were engaged in the
blockade of Bayonne whilst Wellington pushed on towards Toulouse, fighting at
Orthes on the way, Rous's disclosure is still somewhat surprising.

[2] As Wellington approached Toulouse he initially planned to attack from the
south with Hill's corps. A pontoon bridge across the River Garonne was
constructed on March 27th but was found to be too short. Three days later another
was built enabling Hill's 13,000 men to cross. As Rous says, however, he was
recalled owing to the poor state of the water-logged roads.

mind of your old saying, that want of employment is the root of all evil - enough of croaking.

William is posted to the Light Infantry,[3] which I tell him is a great honour. The first picquet he was on, he was struck in the face by a piece of mortar, owing to a round shot striking a house close to him, the wound was not severe enough to leave any mark on the following day. The weather is very fine, as hot as summer. We are not allowed to ride two miles from camp, lest the French should attack us, which is very improbable; we know they are afraid to trust the garrison beyond their outworks. They shot a man who attempted to desert, on the parapet, before us; our sentinels heard two English-men conversing at night in the French lines - most likely they are men who have deserted lately. There is a report that Bonaparte was beaten on the 24th, and that the Allies entered Paris on the 31st;[4] it is a copy of a proclamation from Joseph Bonaparte, which was in a Bordeaux Gazette. There were some doubts as to the circumstance, the Gazette was not dated, and most reports from Bordeaux have proved untrue. My best love to all. Believe me,

Yours very affectionately,

J.E.C. Rous.

---

[3] This is slightly misleading. A British infantry battalion generally consisted of ten companies of which eight were battalion, one was a grenadier, and one a light company. William Rous had not joined another regiment but had, in fact, been posted to the light company of the Coldstream.

[4] The Allies entered Paris on March 31st. Napoleon's 1814 campaign in France has often been regarded as his most dazzling but in the end even he was unable to save his exhausted country from defeat. A combination of ill-luck and betrayals, not to mention the overwhelming odds stacked against him forced a reluctant Napoleon into negotiations with the Allies and on April 6th he abdicated.

ALL SAFE

My Dear Father,   Camp before Bayonne,
                                                   April 16th 1814.

I trust that you will not have heard any report of our loss, before
you receive this letter. William and myself are safe and well after as
severe an attack as I ever recollect. At three o'clock on the morning
of the 14th, the garrison made a false attack on the Spaniards, and at
four attacked us with about half their men, in three columns, two
directed upon the flanks of the picquets taken by the Second Brigade
of Guards, and the other against the village of St Etienne occupied by
Gen. Hay's Brigade of the 5th Division; the picquets behaved
admirably and some of them maintained their posts for nearly half
an hour, till the battalions got under arms, and moved up to their
position. The enemy were in temporary possession of the line
occupied by our picquets, unfortunately the left picquet of the 1st
Brigade, which was on our right, gave up its post by mistake,
fancying they were surrounded, the consequence of which was, that
Gen. Hope was wounded and taken prisoner,[1] and the enemy had
an opportunity of bearing down on our right flank, and forcing our
men to retire with great loss on both sides. Soon after daylight, we
received an order to make a general charge along the line, which was
done in great style, driving the enemy before us, back to their works,
where they formed, and we did the same along our line. Our loss has

---

[1] General Hope was taken when his party was surprised in a hollow by twenty
men of the French 82nd Regiment. The hollow was lined by French infantry
following the unauthorised withdrawal of by a Guards officer of one of the
picquets - mentioned by Rous in his letter. Hope was wounded and his horse shot
dead and despite efforts by two officers he had with him - who were both
wounded - he was taken prisoner. To add insult to injury, Hope was wounded
again by an English bullet while being taken into Bayonne. (Sir W.F.P. Napier,
*History of the War in the Peninsula and in the South of France, from the year 1807 to
the year 1814*. London, Vol. VI. pp.173-174.)

been severe, owing to a great many of the picquets being made prisoners;[2] the loss of the Coldstream is two Officers killed, six wounded, and about 230 or 240 men killed, wounded and prisoners.[3] The loss of the 3rd Regiment is two Officers killed, 3 wounded, and 205 men killed, wounded and prisoners.

	Killed	Wounded[4]
Coldstream.	Lt.Col. Sir H. Sullivan, Capn. Crofton,	Lt.Col. Collier, Capn. Dawkins, Capn. Burroughs, Capn. Harvey, Ens. Pitt, Ens. Vachell,
3rd Reg.	Capn. White, Capn. Shiffner,	Gen. Stopford, Capn. Mahon, Capn. Holbourne.

The four Officers killed were perhaps the best Officers or nearly so, in the Brigade, their deaths will be regretted by everybody who knew them.[5] William was posted in a house with some Light Infantry and

---

[2] Total British casualties were 8 officers and 142 men killed, 36 officers and 419 men wounded and 6 officers and 227 men missing, presumably prisoners: total 838.

[3] Actual Coldstream casualties were 2 officers and 32 men killed, 6 officers and 122 men wounded. (Mackinnon, *Coldstream Guards*, Vol.II. p.202.) The casualty return of the 3rd Guards the morning after lists 35 men killed, 4 officers (2 since dead) and 106 men wounded. One officer and 57 men were listed as missing. (Major General Sir Frederick Maurice, *The History of the Scots Guards*, London, 1934. Vol.I. pp.409-410.)

[4] Of the wounded listed in Rous's letter, Captains Mahon and Holbourne, of the 3rd Guards, and Captain Burroughs and Ensigns Vachell and Pitt, of the Coldstream, subsequently died of their wounds.

[5] Those Guards officers killed in the sortie of April 14th were buried in two small but beautiful cemeteries on the outskirts of Bayonne. The Coldstream Guards Cemetery marks the site of their camp at the time whilst the Scots Guards Cemetery lies in some woods nearby. The latter was tended for many years by the sister of Captain Holbourne of the 3rd Guards fatally wounded on April 14th.

amused himself with firing, and was as cool as a veteran; the rolls of musketry were distinctly heard by our forage party 3 leagues off; the soldiers all say they never recollect so heavy a fire, every gun in the castle on this side was at work, - it is particularly unfortunate, that we only heard yesterday of Peace being signed at Paris and of Marshal Ney having addressed Bonaparte telling him that it was the wish of the people and of the army that the Bourbons should be restored, and peace to be signed.[6]

I received your letter of the 27th yesterday, it gives me the greatest uneasiness to find, that you regret having allowed Anstruther to have gone over my head; it was my fault for having mentioned Hotham's name, and as the army will be in England in a few months it will make no actual difference to me. We shall probably both be reduced as half-pay Captains after the definitive treaty of peace is signed.[7] I think I should prefer travelling through France, to being in Country quarters in Chatham, or living idle in England.

If I should be relieved before we can prevail on the French general to come to amicable terms, I will start for England; if that should not be the case, I shall at least have the pleasure of marching into London with a regiment that has not been in England for five years and a half, and has assisted to drive the French from Lisbon into their own Country, with an army which has proved to the world the superiority of the British arms compared with those of the French, and which by their example have assisted in bringing matters to a crisis so glorious to England, and added to the future welfare of the world. I can only add that it will be doing me the greatest kindness to think no more of having allowed an Officer to go over

---

[6] Napoleon had abdicated on the 6th, eight days before the sortie. Wellington only received the news at Toulouse on April 12th and immediately informed Soult who in turn sent a message to Thouvenot, the Governor of Bayonne. For reasons best known to himself Thouvenot launched the sortie in spite of the fact that he must have known it to be a pointless exercise and a useless waste of life.

[7] The vacancy caused by Hotham's return to England had been filled by Windham Anstruther, over whom Rous had seniority by two weeks. Anstruther, who had been wounded during the Battle of the Nivelle on November 10th became a Lieutenant on March 17th whereas Rous had to wait until May 4th.

my head. With my kindest remembrance to my Mother, believe me to remain,

Your very affectionate Son,

J.E.C. Rous.

The total loss is between 8 and 900 men.
The horses to bring the guns for the siege passed us, but received a counter order in consequence of the news.

ORTHEZ TO TOULOUSE

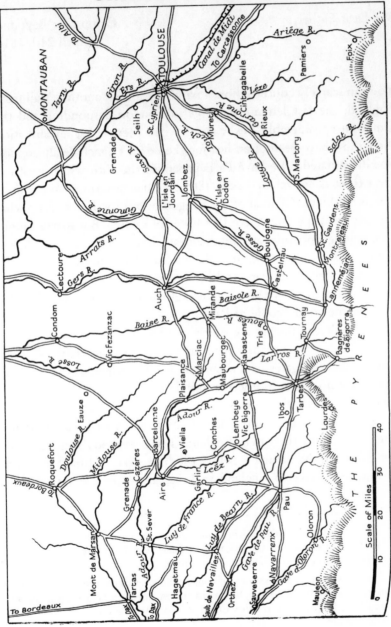

My Dear Father,   Camp near Bayonne,
                                                              April 24th 1814.

You can scarcely conceive how anxious we are for another Mail from
England; the last left most people in London desponding and the
Omnium considerably lower than it had been; what an alteration
there must have been upon hearing the news, I conclude all London
was illuminated.[1] We have Paris papers of the 10th which mention
the expected arrival of Louis 18th, in the meantime Monsieur is
appointed Lieut. General of the Kingdom; but I will not relate what
the English papers have ere this time told you; - Bonaparte cannot
remain long a prisoner at Fontainebleau. The French nation will find
some excuse to try him for his life and hang him;[2] the idea he
mediated of allowing Paris to be plundered for twelve hours, in case
he succeeded in retaking it, is quite sufficient, and shows at once his
love for the good people of Paris.

     Soult and Suchet are nearly the last who have come over to
the new Government, the former sent a letter to the French General
here to open his gates to the English, but the paper was not signed,
and I have no doubt in my own mind that it was an attempt to gain
time, to try whether the soldiers would or would not support
Bonaparte. In two or three days I think we shall be allowed free
intercourse with the town. England is in everybody's mouth; I do
not think we shall embark before the first week in June.[3] It will be
curious if I arrive in England in June; just after our retreat from

---

     [1] The most spectacular celebration came in August 1814 in London and
included a re-enactment of the storming of Badajoz, held in Green Park in front
of a mock castle a hundred and thirty feet high.

     [2] Napoleon escaped execution, of course, and a few days after the sortie from
Bayonne he bid farewell to his Old Guard at Fontainebleau before departing with
around 1,000 followers for the tiny island of Elba where he was to spend his brief -
as it turned out - period of exile.

     [3] The Coldstream did not embark for England until the last week of July.

Burgos everybody told me I should get my promotion in six months; probably you may recollect, that June 1814 was the month was the month I mentioned in one of my letters about that time, to be the month I expected to arrive in England, (a complete prophesy). The Guards ought to be embarked first. What an example we have made of the French Frigates, at the close of the War, it will put the navy in good spirits again.[4]

We are much disappointed at the way in which Lord Wellington mentioned the passage of the Adour by the 1st Division, and the taking of St Etienne; the first was perhaps the most rash act ever attempted by any general, passing over in boats where they had not means to pass more than 1200 men in 24 hours, with a hostile force of 10,000 men within one mile one fifth of which number was perfectly adequate to keep Bayonne from any danger on the other side; he mentions that a Corps of French without saying what their number was attacked us. We well knew the French had above 1200 men opposed to us; we had only seven companies of our Brigade, which his Lordship may call 600 men, but which everybody knows was not more than 500. In the next place he does not mention the German Legion even once,[7] - Perhaps the taking of St Etienne was the most gallant thing ever done. The German Legion consisting of 1600 men took with the bayonet, a strong position, covered with houses every one of which was loop-holed; you may judge of the

---

[4] On March 17th Wellington had asked Admiral Penrose to destroy the shore batteries along the Gironde as well as the French squadron lying there. The squadron consisted of one 80-gun ship, the *Regulus*, three brigs and thirty gunboats. The frigate refused to fight, however, its captain running her ashore while several of the gunboats were either destroyed or captured by the Royal Navy at the cost of just six men. The French later set fire to the frigate and the rest of the ships on April 7th. (Oman, *History of the Peninsular War*, Vol.VII. pp.400-401.)

[7] The German Legion brigades drove the French from St Etienne at bayonet point and suffered 328 casualties doing so. However, Wellington made no mention of the achievement in his despatch which caused much discontent and grumbling amongst its officers. Their senior officer, General Hinüber, who was wounded, complained in a letter but received short shrift from Wellington via Pakenham, his Adjutant-General. (Oman, *History of the Peninsular War*, Vol.VII. p.339.)

praise they deserved when I say they lost 27 Officers, and the distance that his Lordship calls 900 yards from the outworks of the place, is so near that many men can throw a stone from our lines into theirs; the only excuse is he never saw the place, nor was he within 30 miles at the time it was taken. The Germans are much hurt, and everybody who knows their merits, and saw the affair, think they have much reason to be so, - However, we have had enough fighting to suffice everybody.

Capn. Holbourne of the 3rd Guards who was wounded on the 14th died this morning, and Capn. Burroughs of the Coldstream it is supposed cannot live out today; he has been scarcely sensible for some time, the rest with the exception of Mr. Pitt are doing well.[8] With my best love to all, believe me,

Your very affectionate Son,

J.E.C. Rous.

---

[8] Ensign William Pitt died of his wounds on April 24th. Captain William Burroughs died of his wounds on April 26th.

FROM WILLIAM ROUS

My Dear Mother   Camp before Bayonne,
                                        April 24th, 1814.

We are still here, only waiting for our embarkation orders; The Bayonnites have not yet opened their gates but we are in anxious expectation of being admitted as friends in a day or two.[9] Their General, Thouvenot, declares he is very sorry that he ordered the Sortie the other day; it was extremely unlucky as Peace was signed within 48 hours after it.[10] We have lost several very good Officers. I doubt we shall find no purchasers for our animals, the stock will be so numerous and I should think but few purchasers. I am going to Parade. John will finish.

---

[9] Although the war had effectively come to an end on April 12th Thouvenot still refused to surrender Bayonne to the British. Sir John Colville sent him copies of the *Moniteur* and other Parisian papers to convince him that the war was at an end but refused to capitulate until he received an official order. This did not arrive until April 26th when, on receipt of a copy of Soult's armistice, dated the 17th, he finally marched out with his garrison, some 11,800 strong.

[10] Peace was declared two days *before* the sortie.

My Dear Father,   Camp near Bayonne,
                                           June 5th 1814.

I returned here on the 25th Ultimo, much pleased with my trip to
Bordeaux, but was disappointed on my return at not being allowed
to go to England; I told General Howard[1] that I was not only
posted to the 2nd Battalion, but wished to go home as quick as
possible on private business; he in his usual manner without any
reason, refused to forward my leave, for which I am particularly
obliged to him, and mean to take the first opportunity of telling him
so privately. I regret that it will be impossible for me to be present
at Ipswich Races, there being no chance of our embarkation taking
place during the present month.

The Duke of Wellington is at Madrid, but is expected at
Bordeaux on the 10th.[2] The Spanish army breaks up from the
neighbourhood of Toulouse tomorrow, and marches in three
columns, one after the other in successive days on the road to
Bayonne, and from thence to Irun and Vittoria;[3] they will be
followed by the Portuguese army, who are to march through Spain

---

[1] General Kenneth Alexander Howard, 2nd (Coldstream) Guards. Ensign, April
21st 1786; Lieutenant, April 25th 1793; Captain, July 25th 1799; Major, August 4th,
1808. Wounded at St Amand, May 8th 1793. Became a Major-General on July 25th
1810 and commanded a brigade of the 1st Division in the Peninsula.

[2] Wellington was created Duke on May 3rd. He had arrived in Paris the
following day to witness the review of the Allied army there before King Louis
XVIII. On his return south he stopped at Madrid at the request of Lord
Castlereagh to try and help sort out the constitutional problems that had arisen
following the reinstatement of King Ferdinand but left there on June 8th to return
to Bordeaux. According to Stanhope, (*Notes of Conversations with the Duke of
Wellington*, p.19), Wellington passed Soult near Toulouse on the road to Madrid.
As the horses were changed Wellington remained asleep while Soult woke and
spent a short while strolling around the Duke's the carriage, peering through his
spy-glass at Wellington inside.

[3] These were Morillo's Spaniards who, unlike the rest of the Spanish army, had
not been sent home by Wellington the previous November for indiscipline.

to Portugal, passing through Vittoria, Burgos and Salamanca, a long journey to undertake in the hottest part of the year. We shall be sorry to part with the latter; they have been universally such good friends with the English, and are now a very fine army, far better than Portugal ever had before, and infinitely superior to anything Spain can show.[4] The Guards are to embark at Passages, and will be nearly the last.

I was present at a grand Ball given by the inhabitants of Bordeaux to the Duke D'Angouleme which exceeded in splendour and taste anything I ever saw in England. It cost 4000Gs; Supper [was] prepared for 1500 people, and 1600 tickets were issued. The streets are the finest I ever saw, with avenues of trees down the middle, where the company walk from seven to ½ past eight every evening; the outside building of the Theatre is magnificent, the women are pretty, but not so handsome as the English, with better feet and ankles. I am told by people who have been at Paris, that with the exception of the Royal Palace there is nothing to be compared with the town of Bordeaux. William is quite well, we are going to meet twenty-two brother Officers at dinner, to bid farewell to campaigning. I dined with R. Blois twice at Bordeaux. With my best love to all, believe me

Your very affectionate Son,

J.E.C. Rous.

---

[4] The Portuguese soldiers, at first deemed poor and unreliable, had become what Wellington later called, 'the fighting-cocks of the army.' Under the direction of William Beresford the Portuguese had, by the end of the war, gained a reputation equal to that of their British allies who were glad to have them fighting alongside them. They were said to have 'come of age' at Busaco in September 1810 and from then on proved reliable in battle.

OPERATIONS AROUND BORDEAUX
March to April 1814

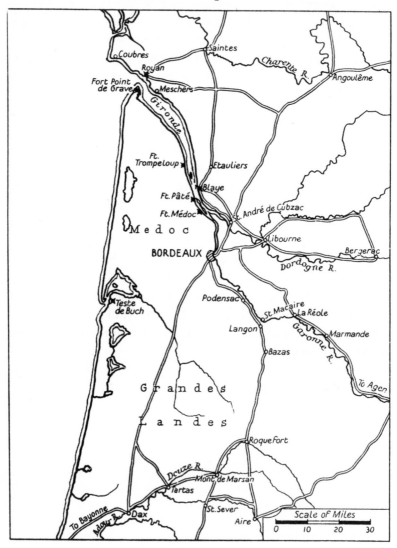

My Dear Mother,

Bordeaux,
July 3rd 1814.

The Guards arrived here on the 23rd of last month, to embark for England but there appears to be no chance of leaving this town before the 10th,[1] which will prevent my arriving in London till after you have left it. This is the best town I ever saw, and since the English have been here the theatre has received such an enormous sum of money, that they have succeeded in drawing off some of the best actors, and dancers from Paris; the French fashion is, to have a Comedy, or Tragedy, and afterwards a Ballet, which is very superior to any Ballet I ever saw at the London Opera, although there is no man who dances better than Vestris.[2] Tonight there is a favourite Ballet for the benefit of a Lady just arrived from Paris. We have very few Balls, and the French do not enter so much into the society of the English, as they did at Toulouse, where it was the fashion always to have an Englishman in every family.

Marshal Suchet comes here with twelve thousand men whenever the English are out of the town; it is lucky he does not come sooner, the French Officers are very much inclined to quarrel, they cannot bear the sight of the English, and take every opportunity of making themselves obnoxious.[3] However, we have had so much the best of it, both with the broadsword and pistol, that they begin

---

[1] Rous's battalion, consisting of 63 sergeants, 69 corporals, 19 drummers and 691 privates, sailed from France just after July 23rd and arrived at Portsmouth on July 28th and marched to London, arriving on August 4th. (Mackinnon, *Coldstream Guards*, Vol.II. p.447.)

[2] Madame Vestris was a famous star of the London Ballet.

[3] This is quite surprising since relations during the Peninsular War between British and French soldiers were very cordial. In fact, there was much fraternisation, particularly between officers or at the outposts with the opposing sides displaying a healthy if grudging respect for each other whereas there was little love lost between the British and their Spanish allies. Relations between the French and Spanish were hostile at best.

to be more civil; they are the most blustering fellows I ever saw, but generally prove great dunghills when they find they cannot bully, in fact whether in the field, or singly it is not possible to draw any comparison between the two nations. It is to be hoped that under the system laid down at present, that a more gentlemanlike set of men will come into the army, and recover their character to what it was considered to be before the reign of Bonaparte. Today I ought to be doing the honours at Ipswich Races, instead of leading an idle life here. With my best love to all, believe me,

Your very affectionate Son,

J.E.C. Rous.

William is pretty well, but is become so fond of Billiards, that you need not expect him to write. I often tell him it will be his ruin, but luckily he does not play for money. A 74[4] arrived last night which says that ten frigates are on their way here.

---

[4] This was the 74-gun ship, *Stirling Castle*, on which the Coldstream sailed for England.

EPILOGUE

The *Stirling Castle*, carrying John Rous and the rest of the 1st Battalion of the Coldstream Guards, arrived at Portsmouth on July 28th. The battalion then marched to London and on August 4th arrived at its barracks in Portman Street. Four days later four companies of the 2nd Battalion of the regiment prepared to march for Ramsgate where they were to embark aboard ships bound for Ostend and from there march to Brussels to join six other companies of the Coldstream already there.

Meanwhile, John Rous, now promoted to the rank of Captain in the 2nd Battalion, departed for Henham for twelve months' leave. However, on February 26th 1815 Napoleon escaped from Elba and entered Paris on March 20th. Rous's sojourn was thus cut short and he was ordered to join his regiment in Brussels. The army with which Wellington had accomplished so much in the Peninsula had been broken up; many soldiers had been paid off whilst many of his veteran battalions had been scattered to various parts of the world, to America for instance from where, as the war there came to a close, his Peninsular veterans were hurrying back to fight Napoleon again. Sadly, the majority arrived too late and Wellington was forced to fight the 1815 campaign in the Low Countries with a mixed army of British, Dutch, Belgians and Germans - 'an infamous army', as he later called it. In fact, many years later John Rous asked the Duke of Wellington what would have happened if he had had his Peninsular veterans at Waterloo and the Duke is alleged to have replied quickly, "It would all have been over in half an hour. I did not dare trust my young soldiers as I could have trusted my old friends."[1]

On March 24th the Coldstream left Brussels for Ath and then marched on to Enghien where the battalion remained until early on the morning of June 16th. By now Napoleon had crossed the Sambre

---

[1] Lady Augusta Fane, *Chit Chat*, London 1926.

and was advancing on the Anglo-Dutch army under Wellington and the Prussian army under Marshal Blucher. The Coldstream marched from Enghien at three o'clock in the morning of the 16th and after a fatiguing march of twenty-five miles reached Quatre Bras at about four in the afternoon. The Coldstream was immediately thrown into the battle in support of the 1st Foot Guards who had arrived earlier.

It was at Quatre Bras that John Rous was wounded. Some say that he was shot in the leg but others report that he was on a recce with his Colonel when his horse fell on him and fractured his hip. Another memoir claims that a few hours before the famous Waterloo Ball, given by the Duke of Richmond, he was riding out of the city when his horse stumbled and fell, and he suffered an 'ugly' fracture of the leg.[2] Whatever the cause, he was unable to take part in the memorable Battle of Waterloo, fought on June 18th.[3] On that fateful day the Coldstream played a major part in the battle when, along with the 3rd Foot Guards, it held the vital position of the chateau of Hougoumont against repeated French attacks. Indeed, Wellington had told Lieutenant Colonel Macdonell, of the Coldstream, commanding the Guards at the chateau, to 'defend the post to the last extremity,' and when the French broke into the courtyard it looked as if they might have to. However, Macdonell rushed to the gate with a group of officers and men and putting their shoulders to it managed to close it. Those French soldiers still inside were quickly hunted down until all but a young drummer boy was either killed or driven out. The importance of this action was borne out by a statement by Wellington himself who later said, 'The outcome of the day depended on the closing of the gates at Hougoumont.' The fight for Hougoumont - originally intended by Napoleon as a diversionary attack - became a battle in itself as thousands of French troops, commanded by Prince Jerome Bonaparte, were swallowed up in the futile attacks on the chateau and who might otherwise have been

---

[2] The *Ipswich Journal*, Saturday, January 30th 1886.
[3] Rous' name is indeed missing from the Coldstreamers present at Waterloo. His company may possibly have been the 5th company, which was commanded on the day by Ensign Robert Bowen.

used elsewhere during the day. John Rous, meanwhile, was bed-ridden in Brussels but learned of the great victory when an ecstatic Duke of Richmond burst into his room on the evening of the 18th to tell him the good news.

Many years later, in 1878, Colonel Freemantle was in the chair during a meeting of the Coldstream Guards Officers' Dining Club[4] when he proposed a toast to the oldest Coldstreamer in the room, who happened to be John Rous, by then, of course, the Earl of Stradbroke. Getting to his feet, the Earl replied, "I am also very proud to have been present with the regiment at the famous battle of Quatre Bras, but unfortunately I was wounded and so was unable to be present at the much more famous battle the following day - I mean the battle at which the great Duke of Wellington commanded the Allied Army when it defeated the French under the Emperor Napoleon. But you must excuse a temporary lapse of memory by an old man, for I cannot remember its name." And when someone said, 'Waterloo,' the Earl exclaimed, "Waterloo - of course, Waterloo! How foolish of me not to remember."[5]

John Rous stayed with the Coldstream Guards for three more years before returning to Henham in 1818. For many years afterwards his name was associated with the East Suffolk Light Infantry Militia. He was gazetted Colonel in May 1830 when the County Reserve was divided and the Duke of Grafton appointed to the command of the West Suffolk Battalion. In fact, Rous only severed his connection with the forces on his appointment in 1844 to the Lord Lieutenancy of the county. Four years later he was among the recipients of the General Service Medal with clasps for Salamanca, Vittoria, the Nive and Nivelle.

In 1827 he had succeeded his father to become the 2nd Earl of Stradbroke. He inherited Henham Hall and its substantial Estate

---

[4] This dining club is called the 'Nulli Club', after the Coldstream Guards' motto, *Nulli Secundus* (Second to None).

[5] *Men and Women and Things*, Memories of the Duke of Rutland, London 1937, and also recounted in 'On Old Guardsman', in *Jottings in a General's Notebook*, by Michael Gow, London 1989, p.17.

as well as, among other things, a stud of thoroughbred horses and a kennel of greyhounds. The stud was famous for breeding successful racehorses, but John Rous took a far greater interest in breeding than racing, unlike his brother Admiral The Honourable Henry John Rous who, following a distinguished naval career, devoted the remaining forty years of his life to racing and was often referred to as 'the Dictator of the Turf'.[6] John Rous' greyhounds were perhaps even more celebrated than his horses and between 1835 and 1850 his kennels produced some of the most famous winners in England.

John Rous had a great many interests and was a very busy man all his life. He was a keen and knowledgeable agriculturalist and he helped his tenant farmers through the bad times of 1830 to 1840 when there was a severs crisis in agriculture. He devoted much of his life to politics. He was born and bred a Conservative, but did not always see eye to eye with his party and he was one of the peers who voted for the repeal of the Corn Laws. When the railroads were first built he advocated that they should be owned by the State, arguing that they would bring in great revenues which could eventually pay off the National Debt.

On May 26th 1857, at the age of sixty-three, he married Mrs Augusta Bonham, second daughter of the Reverend Sir Christopher Musgrave of Edenhall and the widow of Colonel Bonham - of Bonham's auctioneers fame - of the 10th Hussars. Mrs Bonham arrived with three children by her first marriage and six more - a son and five daughters - were to follow! No children ever enjoyed a more delightful home than Henham, a huge house with plenty of servants and surrounded by its spacious Repton landscaped park. There were

---

[6] During the Admiral's naval career, his most colourful feat was to bring safely home the battered frigate, *Pique*, which had been grounded off the coast of Newfoundland. In an extraordinary time of twenty days he guided, cajoled and coerced his rudderless ship without keel or pump, leaking two feet of water an hour, the 1,500 mile journey back home. The reason he gave the Admiralty for this haste was that he had to be at Newmarket for the races! The action earned him a court martial but he was acquitted and commended for his seamanship. The Rous family possesses a fine oil painting which shows the *Pique* in heavy seas with its improvised rudder.

ponies and dogs galore and a father who took a great interest in his children right up to his death in 1886. His children would listen intensely as many an evening was enlivened with tales of the Earl's adventures in the Peninsula. "In one of the battles," he was said, "the shells were flying all around us, and I and a private got into a ditch together. While we were lying there - my head one way and the private's the other - a shot passed right over my head and struck the head of the private, killing him on the spot, but not injuring me."[7]

The weight of the years began to take their toll but although there was a decline in the Earl's physical condition his intellect continued unimpaired and his interest in public affairs remained unabated. Towards the end of 1885, however, he contracted a slight cold which developed into bronchitis. On the evening of January 27th, his son, Viscount Dunwich, occupied the chair for the meeting of the Estate rent audit when a messenger arrived with news of his father's sudden deterioration. He departed hastily for Henham Hall where the Countess of Stradbroke, Lady Sophia, Lady Hilda and Lady Gwendolin Rous were already gathered. When he arrived at Henham, however, he was told that his father had passed away peacefully at 9.30 pm. He was two weeks away from his ninety-second birthday.

John Rous was laid to rest in the Parish Church at Wangford in Suffolk with all the stateliness and dignity as befits a hero of the Peninsula and a man who was called 'the central figure of county administration for a period approaching half a century.' He had led a remarkable life, as a soldier, a family man and as a distinguished servant not only of the County of Suffolk but also of his country and he would have been proud of his descendants who have continued the family traditions. His son George, the 3rd Earl, served in the Army, was Governor of Victoria and later became Lord Lieutenant of Suffolk. His grandson John, the 4th Earl, served in the Royal Navy and was in turn Lord Lieutenant of Suffolk. His other grandsons were Keith, the 5th Earl, who served in the Royal Navy,

---

[7] The *Ipswich Journal*, January 30th 1886.

George in The Life Guards, and Peter in the 16th/5th The Queen's Royal Lancers.

His great grandson Keith, the 6th Earl, has spent much of his life in Australia but now lives at Henham and plans to rebuild a mansion in the Park to replace the Hall which was demolished in 1953.[8] The 6th Earl's younger brother, William, who has graced this book with his Foreword, has followed his great grandfather into the Coldstream Guards and is still serving. And in turn, his son James - John Rous' great great grandson - has just joined the Regiment, thus maintaining a proud family tradition stretching back to 1810, to John Rous, a Guards Officer in the Peninsula.

---

[8] Henham Hall was used as a hospital in World War I and during World War II was used as a barracks.

APPENDIX I

Officers of the First Battalion of the Coldstream Guards in the Peninsula from January to December 1812

(January 1st to December 31st unless otherwise stated.)

COLONELS

Joseph Fuller
> *January 1st to May 31st. Posted to 2nd Batt. June 1st 1812*

LIEUTENANT COLONELS

Hon. Henry Brand
> *June to October 6th 1812. Sick leave, England from October 7th 1812. Posted to 2nd Batt. January 1st 1813.*

James Philips
> *Joined 2nd Batt. December 1812.*

Sir Gilbert Stirling, Bart.
> *January 1st to February 28th. Retired, March 1st 1812.*

Alexander Woodford
James Macdonnell
> *May to December 31st.*

CAPTAINS

Lucius Frederick Adams
> *Promoted to 2nd Batt. April 1812.*

William Henley Raikes
> *January 1st to January 26th, August to December 31st. Sick leave, England, January 27th to August 1812.*

Thomas Barrow
>   *January 1st to February 9th, July to December 31st. Leave, England, February 10th to July.*

Hon. William George Crofton

Daniel Mackinnon
>   *June to September. Recruiting, England, January 1st to May and September to December 31st.*

Hon. John Walpole
>   *January 1st to November 19th. Leave, England, November 20th.*

Thomas Steele

Edward Harvey
>   *January 1st to October 18th. Killed Burgos, October 18th.*

William Burroughs
>   *July to December 31st.*

George Bowles

Thomas Sowerby

Edward Lascelles

Patrick Sandilands

John Freemantle
>   *January 1st to November. ADC to Wellington, November.*

Charles MacKenzie Fraser
>   *May to October 5th. Sick, wounded, England, October 6th.*

ENSIGNS

Charles White
>   *January 1st to April. Joined 2nd Batt. on promotion, April.*

Thomas Bligh
>   *January 1st to April. Joined 2nd Batt. on promotion, April.*

Charles Shawe
>   *January 1st to June 3rd. Joined 2nd Batt. on promotion June 4th.*

George Henry Macartney Greville
>   *January 1st to November 1st. Joined 2nd Batt. on promotion November 2nd.*

John Talbot
George Harvey Percival
Walter George Baynes
John Stepney Cowell
Wentworth Noel Burgess
        January 1st to October 18th. Killed Burgos, October 18th.
John Mills
James Bradshaw
        January 1st to October 28th. Joined 2nd Batt. October 29th.
Francis Love Beckford
        January 1st to October 3rd, Sick leave, England, October 4th.
John Charles Buckeridge
        May to October 7th. Killed Burgos, October 7th.
John Lucie Blackman
        April to December 31st.
William Grimstead
        April to October 3rd. Leave, England, October 4th.
Beaumont, Lord Hotham
        April to July 22nd, November 30th to December 31st. Sick,
        wounded, July 23rd to November 29th.
Hon. John Rous
        July to December 31st.
Windham Anstruther
        June to December 31st.
Charles Shirley
        December to December 31st.
Frederick Vachell

QUARTERMASTERS ▦▦▦▦▦▦▦▦▦▦

John Holmes
        January 1st to May 8th. Joined 2nd Batt. May 9th.
Thomas Dwelley
        October 15th to December 27th. Joined 2nd Batt. December 28th.

ASSISTANT SURGEONS

Thomas Rose
> *January 1st to October 5th. Leave, England, October 6th.*

Edward Nixon
> *January 1st to December 3rd. Leave, England, December 4th.*

Thomas Maynard
> *October to December 31st.*

APPENDIX II

Officers of the First Battalion of the Coldstream Guards in the Peninsula from January to December 1813

(January 1st to December 31st unless otherwise stated.)

LIEUTENANT COLONELS

Alexander Woodford
James Macdonnell
George Collier
John Hamilton
> *July to December 31st.*

CAPTAINS

William Henley Raikes
> *January 1st to May 16th. Sick leave, England, May 18th. Posted to 2nd Batt. July.*

Thomas Gore
> *March to December 31st.*

Thomas Barrow (Major)
> *January 1st to December 22nd. Leave, England, December 23rd.*

Hon. William George Crofton
Thomas Steele
William Burroughs
George Bowles
Thomas Sowerby
Edward Lascelles (Adjutant)
Patrick Sandilands

John Freemantle
> *ADC to Wellington, January 1st to December 31st.*

John Prince

James Vigours Harvey
> *July to Decmber 31st.*

ENSIGNS

George Harvey Percival
> *January 1st to March 14th. Joined 2nd Batt. March 15th.*

Walter George Baynes
> *January 1st to July 21st. To England on promotion, July 22nd.*

John Stepney Cowell
> *January 1st to October. To England on promotion, October.*

John Mills
> *January 1st to 31st. Leave to England, February.*

John Lucie Blackman

Beaumont, Lord Hotham

Hon. John Rous

Windham Anstruther

Charles Shirley

John Drummond

Hon. Robert Moore

Charles Andrew Giradot

Thomas Chaplin
> *May to September 26th. Wounded, to England, September 27th.*

Edward Clifton
> *July to December 31st.*

Henry Salwey
> *September to December 31st.*

George Gould Morgan
> *September to December 31st.*

Frederick Vachell

William Kortright

QUARTERMASTERS

Benjamin Selway

SURGEON

Thomas Rose
July to December 31st.

ASSISTANT SURGEONS

William Whymper
June to December 31st.
Thomas Maynard

APPENDIX III

Officers of the First Battalion of the Coldstream Guards in the Peninsula from January to July 1814

(January to July unless otherwise stated.)

LIEUTENANT COLONELS

Alexander Woodford
James Macdonnell
January 1st to 31st. Ordered to Holland, February 1st.
George Collier
January 1st to May 10th. Died of his wounds, May 10th.
John Hamilton
Sir Henry Sullivan, Bart.
March to April 14th. Killed at Bayonne, April 14th.
Thomas Gore
January 1st to February 11th. Joined 2nd Batt. on promotion, February 12th.

CAPTAINS

Hon. William George Crofton
January 1st to April 14th. Killed at Bayonne, April 14th.
Thomas Steele
William Burroughs
January 1st to April 26th. Died of his wounds, April 26th.
George Bowles
Thomas Sowerby
Edward Lascelles (Adjutant)
Patrick Sandilands

John Prince
> *January 1st to January 9th. Leave to England, January 10th.*

James Vigours Harvey
> *January 1st to June. Sick, wounded to England, June.*

John Freemantle (Major)
> *ADC to Wellington, January 1st to July.*

ENSIGNS

John Lucie Blackman
> *January 1st to April 4th. Joined 2nd Batt. on promotion, April 5th.*

Beaumont, Lord Hotham
> *January 1st to February. Joined 2nd batt. on promotion, February.*

Hon. John Rous
> *January 1st to May. Joined 2nd Batt. on promotion, June.*

Windham Anstruther
> *January 1st to February 13th. Sick, wounded, to England. February 14th.*

Charles Shirley
> *January 1st to June 8th. Joined 2nd Batt. on promotion June 9th.*

John Drummond

Hon. Robert Moore

Charles Andrew Giradot

Edward Clifton

Henry Salwey

George Gould Morgan

Frederick Vachell
> *January 1st to May 13th. Died of his wounds, May 13th.*

Hon. James Forbes
> *March to July. With 2nd Batt. January to February.*

William Pitt
> *January 1st to April 24th. Died of his wounds, 24th April.*

William Kortright
Henry Armytage
    March to July.
Hon. William Rufus Rous
    March to July.
Henry John William Bentinck
    April to July.

QUARTERMASTERS

Benjamin Selway

SURGEON

Thomas Rose
    January 1st to June. To England in charge of sick, June to July.

ASSISTANT SURGEONS

William Whymper
    January 1st to January 4th. Leave to England, January 5th.
Thomas Maynard

APPENDIX IV

THE EARL OF STRADBROKE.

(Re-printed from 'Vanity Fair' of July 31st 1875, Statesmen, No. 209.)

John Edward Cornwallis Rous, second Earl of Stradbroke, brother to the Admiral, has lived a long life in stirring times. Sprung from a family which was ancient and possessing the soil of Suffolk before the modern nobility was invented, heir to an estate which had descended lineally in his family from the time of Edward III, and with the traditions of a great-grandfather who had sacrificed his goods and barely saved his life in the cause of Charles I, the boy became a Guardsman at sixteen, and before he was twenty had the good fortune to take part in those campaigns against Napoleon upon which the prestige of the British army now rests. A man who was at Salamanca and Vittoria, and who still bears in a broken hip-bone a glorious mark of the field of Waterloo, may fairly claim to have seen service, and the Rouses, who have been a gallant race of gentlemen since the days of the Conqueror, had every reason to be proud of their young soldier. But having served his country, he sold out soon after the peace and took to serving his county. He became a magistrate, he succeeded his father in the Peerage, he was made Lord Lieutenant and Vice-Admiral of Suffolk, and after being the chief magnate of that county for many years he had his reward in marrying for his wife a charming, energetic and active-minded lady, who has still further distinguished his name in all the departments of rural economy, and has made all his houses most desirable places of resort. A devoted Conservative and an intimate friend of the late Lord Derby he is yet a man of liberal mind and eager progress, so that he voted for Catholic emancipation and the first Reform Bill, and has consistently refused to accept from his Party any favour or salaried post. So shrewd and practical man of business as to have been chosen as arbitrator in the dispute over the late Lord Hertford's property, so great an authority on the Poor Laws as to have been for upwards of forty years Chairman of the Local Board, so good a judge of a horse as to be preferred by many in that capacity to his brother, a professor of coursing and a capital shot, and having withal the high breeding and manner of the gentlemen of the old school, he commands respect throughout his county. He is the patron of six livings. Being of a vigorous and vivacious race, he has taken and still - when over one-and-eighty and a victim to gout - takes a considerable interest in the public business of the Lords. His intellect is as clear and his memory as unfailing as ever, and in all his acts and ways he is the type of the better kind of man that the best blood in England has produced.

SELECT BIBLIOGRAPHY

As most of the works used in writing this book are to be found listed in the footnotes, I have included in this bibliography only general histories of the Peninsular War or those books concerned with Wellington's army and in particular, of course, his Foot Guards.

Aubrey-Fletcher, Major H.L. *A History of the Foot Guards to 1856.* London, 1927.

Bentley, Nicholas, (ed.) *Selections from the Reminiscences of Captain Gronow.* London, 1977.

Brett-James, Anthony. *Life in Wellington's Army.* London, 1972.

Davies, Godfrey, *Wellington and His Army.* London, 1954.

Fortescue, Hon. J.W. *History of the British Army. 13 Vols.* London, 1910-1930.

Hamilton, Lt.Gen. Sir F.W. *The Origin and History of the First or Grenadier Guards.* 3 Vols. London, 1874.

Mackinnon, Colonel Daniel. *Origins and Services of the Coldstream Guards. Vol.2.* London, 1833.

Malmesbury, Earl of. *A Series of Letters of the First Earl of Malmesbury, his Family and Friends from 1745 to 1820.* London, 1870.

Napier, Sir W.F.P. *History of the War in the Peninsula and in the South of France, From the Year 1807 to 1814. 6 Vols.* London, 1876.

Oman, Sir Charles. *A History of the Peninsular War. 7 Vols.* Oxford, 1902-1930.

Stanhope, Philip Henry. *Notes of Conversations with the Duke of Wellington.* London, 1888.

Wellington, Arthur Wellesley, 1st Duke of. (edited Gurwood) *The Despatches of Field Marshal the Duke of Wellington, during his Various Campaigns in India, Denmark, Portugal, the Low Countries and France, from 1799-1818. 13 Volumes.* London, 1837-39.

INDEX